Echoes of Eternity:

A Classical Guide to
MUSIC

Stephen R. Turley, PhD

Series Editor: Stephen R. Turley, PhD

Echoes of Eternity:
A Classical Guide to Music
© Classical Academic Press, 2018
Version 1.0

ISBN: 978-1-60051-344-2

Cover by Lenora Riley
Layout by Lauraine Gustafson

Classical Academic Press
515 S. 32nd Street
Camp Hill, PA 17011
www.ClassicalAcademicPress.com

PGP.06.18

To my dear wife, Akiko, whose music and beauty
have graced my life for only thirty years.

TABLE OF CONTENTS

Prelude. ix

Part I: Sound as Revelation

CHAPTER ONE. Life Is Beautiful: Music as Revelation 1

1. Discoveries in a Sonic Garden. .1

2. The World of Sound and the Eclipse of the Visual. 2

3. Faith Comes by Hearing. 5

4. Music as Aural Sacrament. 6

    Questions for Reflection and Discussion 8

    Suggested Listening Exercises. 9

    Suggestions for Further Reading. 9

CHAPTER TWO. Soundscapes: Making Sonic Sense. 11

1. Introduction. 11

2. The World of Sound. 12

3. The Visible Invisible and the Hearing Body. 13

4. Encountering the World of Sounds. 15

5. Auditory Fields and the Numinous. 18

6. Summary. 20

    Questions for Reflection and Discussion 20

    Suggested Listening Exercise. 21

    Suggestions for Further Reading. 21

Part II: Echoes of Eternity

**Chapter Three. What Is Music?
Exploring the World of Song** **25**

1. Introduction 25

2. Defining Music 26

3. Meaning and Music 27

4. The Features of Music: Revelation of Sonic Worlds 29

5. Music and the Numinous 42

6. Summary 43

   Questions for Reflection and Discussion 44

   Suggested Listening Exercise 45

   Suggestions for Further Reading 45

**Chapter Four. The Melody of Creation:
Music as Cosmic Song** **47**

1. Introduction 47

2. Musical Relativism 47

3. From Creation to Nature 50

4. The Music of Creation 51

5. The Music of the Spheres 52

6. The Christian Reappropriation 54

7. Music and the Sanctification of the Soul 55

8. Music: Then and Now 58

9. Summary 59

   Questions for Reflection and Discussion 60

   Suggested Listening Exercise 61

   Suggestions for Further Reading 61

**Chapter Five. The Song of the Seraphim:
Music as Echoes of Paradise** **63**

1. Introduction 63

2. The Sounds of Paradise 64

3. The Heralds of Heaven: The Soundscape of the Church 67

4. Summary 72

    Questions for Reflection and Discussion 72

    Suggested Listening Exercise. 73

    Suggestions for Further Reading. 73

**CHAPTER SIX. Rock 'n' Roll Music and the Church:
A Morally Ambiguous Reunion** **75**

1. Introduction 75

2. CCM and Secular Culture 76

3. The Church of Rock 77

4. The Rock 'n' Roll Body .79

5. Contemporary Christian Music:
    An Ambiguous Reunion 80

6. Privatized Space, Personal Faith. 81

7. Redeeming CCM 83

    Questions for Reflection and Discussion 85

    Suggested Listening Exercise. 86

    Suggestions for Further Reading. 86

CHAPTER SEVEN. Echoes of Eternity: Summary **87**

Part III: Music Practice

**CHAPTER EIGHT. The Art of Listening:
The Practical Aesthetics of Music** **91**

1. Introduction 91

2. Musical Analysis 92

3. The Sounds of Spring 93

4. The Architecture of Analysis 95

5. Summary 102

    Questions for Reflection and Discussion 102

    Suggested Listening Exercise. 103

    Suggestions for Further Reading. 103

**Chapter Nine. O 'Twas a Joyful Sound We Hear:
On Singing Psalms** 105

  1. Introduction 105

  2. The Summary of Scripture 107

  3. Christ's Own Prayers. 108

  4. Harmony of the Soul 109

  5. Psalmody and Christian Culture 110

  6. A New Generation of Psalm Singers 112

     Questions for Reflection and Discussion 113

     Suggested Listening Exercises 114

     Suggestions for Further Reading. 114

Postlude 117

**Appendix A: Seven Ways to Incorporate Music
throughout the School Day** 119

**Appendix B: Time and Eternity:
The Sacred Soundscape of Arvo Pärt** 123

Bibliography 127

About the Author 133

PRELUDE

This book has been a long time coming. First, as a classical guitar performance major, I spent more than eight years of my life at one of the finest music conservatories in the world. Before that, I traveled each Saturday ten hours by train round-trip from New Haven, CT, to Baltimore, MD, to study classical guitar with a master teacher in preparation for my future conservatory years. Those years would include prizes in music competitions and performances on television and in concert halls throughout the United States, as well as Italy and Japan.

And yet it was not until much later in life that I began to reflect on the profound significance of music for the formation of our humanity. While I had always loved music, I am embarrassed to admit that as a performance artist I was more interested in my public persona than my art. Ironically, it was only when I put down the guitar to pursue a teaching career in classical education that the real magnitude of music impressed itself upon me.

Which brings me to the second reason for the protraction of this publication: the long-awaited arrival of its readership. The renewal of classical education over the last few decades affords the opportunity for many of us to rediscover the *classical* notion of music. By "classical," I'm not referring solely to the music genre by that name, much less to the term used by musicologists and historians to specify that musical period between the mid-eighteenth to early nineteenth centuries. Instead, I mean the conception and practice of music that echoed a universe full of divine meaning and purpose, a cosmos that resonated with stunning correspondences and grand harmonies that became audible in music making and composition.

We in the modern world, so devoted to scientific reasoning and technological progress, have lost largely the mystical meaning of music that accounted for its once formative power. In Jewish, Greek, and Christian traditions, music revealed the world as an arena of divine creation, comprised of symmetries, consonances, and harmonies. By awakening the music of the heavens on earth through the contemplation of divine revelation, we were able to embody such cosmic harmony and thereby transform into heavenly beings. Music was thus deemed integral to the formation of what it meant to be truly human, and was therefore considered a kind of knowledge indispensable to such formation.

As classical educators, administrators, and parents, we often find ourselves at a loss for communicating such a vision of music to our students. In an age of iPods and iPads, commodification and consumerism has redefined not only the world of music, but also the world as expressed and interpreted by music. It is virtually unthinkable among us to hear our Top 40 hits as echoes of a cosmos resonating with divine harmonies, and attempts at teaching such on the part of the educator appear artificially forced if not unintelligible.

This book was written to resolve such obstacles. Its pages provide a rich tapestry of concepts, vocabulary, and listening examples that will equip you to teach and awaken students to a classical vision of music. There is no formal musical education required on your part; while music teachers can certainly benefit from its contents, this book is purposely written with both musicians and nonmusicians in mind. By reading this book, you will be able to:

- discover and express a rich theology of music and music practice;

- explain effectively how the value of music is objective to the listener;

- clarify the difference between classical and contemporary music;

- demonstrate how to analyze music and musical meaning;

- learn ways to incorporate music throughout the school day;

- explain the multiple ways in which music communicates through various cross-cultural examples;

- understand the significance of sound for our human experience.

I have organized the book into three parts. Part I: Sound as Revelation explores music in relation to the larger issue of the significance of sound for our human experience. Chapter 1 provides an overview of the historic role of hearing and music in shaping our conceptions of what it means to be human, while chapter 2 explores the profound contribution of sound to our perception of the world, particularly as it relates to a thoroughly mystical notion of reality.

Part II: Echoes of Eternity details what I consider to be indispensable to a rich theology of music. Chapter 3 delineates the unique properties or traits of music that account for its capacity to reveal unseen and otherwise imperceptible realities, which in turn accounts for the mystical sense ascribed to music by cultures throughout the world. In chapter 4, we rediscover the ancient conception of the music of the spheres and its relation to the formation of wisdom and virtue in the listener, and in chapter 5 I sketch a distinctively Christian theology of music from the writings of the early church. Chapter 6 reflects on the moral ambiguity in contemporary Christian music, while chapter 7 provides a summary of the constituents of a theology of music.

Part III: Music Practice finishes our rediscovery with two chapters dedicated to applying our music theology to the analysis, appreciation, and performance of music. Chapter 8 provides an interpretive grid for an aesthetic analysis of music, and chapter 9 expounds on the significance of psalm singing for the Christian life. After a brief postlude, I've included two appendices that continue with the theme of music practice. The first suggests ways to incorporate music in the classroom throughout the school day, and the second introduces readers to the life and music of the Estonian composer Arvo Pärt, whom many consider to be the greatest living composer in our time.

All chapters include discussion questions, at least one suggested listening exercise, and a suggested reading list.

And so, this book is in many respects a culmination of a life of music and classical education. As you, the reader, turn its pages, it is my hope that you will glean from its words the profound significance of song for the realization of our humanity. I desire nothing less than to inspire you to make the same discovery that has so astonished me, to encounter the melodies of redemption that interweave into sonic harmonies that hearken us back to the sounds of Paradise, that awaken us to the echoes of eternity, leading us back to our original and eternal home.

Part I
Sound as Revelation

CHAPTER ONE
Life Is Beautiful: Music as Revelation

1. DISCOVERIES IN A SONIC GARDEN

I began playing guitar at the age of twelve, shortly after my father died. His death had a devastating effect on me. I withdrew from all the sporting events in which I was involved, and I became more and more secluded from friends and activities. My mother, in an effort to persuade me to be more outgoing, suggested that I learn to do something constructive, such as play an instrument. I then remembered how I had always wanted to play the guitar.

My love for music was fostered by my paternal grandfather, Harold G. Turley, who emigrated from England in the early 1920s as the first full-time research chemist for Rohm and Haas. He settled with his wife, Cecilia, and four children in a large, stone-front Dutch colonial home in Moorestown, NJ. My cousins called the home "the castle," for it was in fact an inexhaustible treasure trove of stairwells, pantries, attic spaces, books, and basement that awakened a veritable Narnia within our childlike imaginations. And it was there, in that magical cottage, with guitar in hand absent my father's touch, that I discovered music.

My grandfather devoted his retirement years to two things: rose gardening and listening to classical music. As I settle into midlife, I recognize more and more the profound sympathy between these two practices. The invisible fragrance of the garden in a very real way becomes audible through the comparably invisible waves of melodies, which intertwine in harmony with the symphony of scents from the bouquet of blossoming flowers. Like gardening, music finds its life in time; it wraps itself up with calendrical seasons and chapters of life, marking rites of passage from birthdays to graduations, weddings to funerals. Its sonic perfume breathes into our innermost beings, imprinting itself in our minds and resounding in our imaginations, and attaches itself to our bodies, sanctifying our senses with a seemingly inexhaustible source of ineluctable delight.

2. THE WORLD OF SOUND AND THE ECLIPSE OF THE VISUAL

I have come to appreciate that the world of sound is both a unique and indispensable dimension of our humanity. While sight is directional, in that my visual experience of the world is limited to where my eyes are looking, hearing is omnidirectional. The world of sound surrounds and envelops me; it is in front of me and behind me, left and right, above and below. As theologian John Hull has written, sound is "a world which I cannot shut out, which goes on all around me, and which gets on with its own life. . . . Acoustic space is a world of revelation."[1]

Unfortunately, the world of sound has been largely neglected by our contemporary culture. We together live in what is called the modern age, which for us in the West means that we live on the other side of that intellectual and technological revolution known as the Enlightenment. The Enlightenment was and remains a Western worldview that enthroned science and reason as the principal methods by which we know our world, a knowledge entailing a supposed unprecedented degree of certainty. However, for all of its commitment to objectivity, scholars have noted that the Western

1. John Hull, *Touching the Rock: An Experience of Blindness* (London: SPCK, 1990), 61–64; as cited in Jeremy S. Begbie, *Theology, Music and Time* (Cambridge: Cambridge University Press, 2000), 25.

   Chapter One. Life Is Beautiful: Music as Revelation

obsession with empirical evidence *emphasizes the visual,* generating its own biases—what might be called "visualism." Western thought reflects a deep ideological partiality toward vision as the "noblest sense," the visual representing the most exact way of communicating knowledge.[2] The famous dictum of the eighteenth-century British philosopher John Locke summarizes well this bias: "The perception of the mind is most aptly explained by words relating to the sight."[3]

> *When it comes to the fundamental and lasting questions of life . . . these are questions that cannot be answered by balance sheets, flowcharts, or user's manuals; these are questions that can only be answered by* listening, *specifically listening to what God has said and continues to say.*

With the advent of photography, advertising, television, and computer graphics, there has been a clear triumph of the visional in Western culture. There is today a subtle yet pronounced conceptual link established between image and reality, indicated by idioms such as "image is everything" and "seeing is believing," or the importance of "eyewitness testimony" in the courtroom. In contrast, we never say "sound is everything" or "hearing is believing."[4]

I am more and more convinced that this emphasis on the visual has had a profound effect on how we relate to the world, particularly with respect to our conception of *knowledge*: if we can *see* the

---

2. Johannes Fabian, *Time and the Other: How Anthropology Makes Its Object* (New York: Columbia University Press, 1983), 106.

3. Cited in Guy L. Beck, *Sonic Theology: Hinduism and Sacred Sound* (Columbia: University of South Carolina Press, 1993), 1.

4. And yet, as my colleague Bill Stutzman points out, we've never been more surrounded by sound; music constantly plays in our public spaces, through our earbuds, in our cars, etc. We actually are so accustomed to it that we have trained ourselves to tune it out and *not* hear. Always hearing, we don't hear.

relationships between things, such as a flowchart, lab report, or user's manual, we believe that we can have a better understanding of things than if they were communicated through another medium, such as a song or poem. We live in a world where balance sheets, not Bach, reveal reality.

But this prejudice tends to eclipse another way of imagining our world and what it means to know within it. When it comes to the fundamental and lasting questions of life, such as what it means to be human, what it means to have purpose and significance, and what it means to exist, these are questions that cannot be answered by balance sheets, flowcharts, or user's manuals; these are questions that can only be answered by *listening*, specifically listening to what God has said and continues to say. Hence, in Greek, the word "to hear" (*akouein*) also means "to obey."

Perhaps you might be familiar with Walker Percy's parable "The Message in the Bottle." He wrote of a castaway with amnesia stranded on an island. As he assimilates with the natives of the island, he begins to realize that their scientific and analytical way of understanding the world cannot account for or answer the question of why he was on the island to begin with. In order for him to discover who he is, he must receive news from across the sea.

Percy's parable is about us. We find ourselves on this third rock from the sun, surrounded by a sea of cosmic space, and the only possible way that we can know why we are here and what life really means is if a voice from outside this cosmos breaks in and tells us. Science and technology can't help us here; we have to be open to another way of knowing, which comes only through listening.

3. Faith Comes by Hearing

I therefore find it fascinating that in our Christian tradition, we are designated by St. Paul as the *klētos* or "called ones," who belong to the *ekklesia,* the Greek word for "church," which is a combination of *ek,* meaning "out of," and *kalein,* meaning "to call." A call is something audible, something meant to be heard and received, not simply seen or read. The church is constituted by those who have been "called out of" or "called forth" from the world in order to gather together and witness to the breaking in of another world. In Romans 10:14-17, Paul asks, "How will they believe in Him whom they have not heard? . . . Just as it is written, 'How beautiful are the feet of those who bring good news of good things!' . . . So faith comes from *hearing*" (NASB, emphasis added).

And so there is present throughout the history of Christian thought a sense that the redemption of the cosmos in Christ is revealed and thereby known through music, *the ways in which Christianity* sounds.

It was within this sonic world that a distinctly Christian soundscape emerged. This Christocentric soundscape, empowered by the Holy Spirit, set the stage for what patristics scholar Carol Harrison has called "transformative listening." Christian rhetoric, embodied in the sermon or homily, combined with sacred chant in order to awaken the imagination through sound, inspiring the listener not merely to hear but also to understand, to apprehend Scripture as it was combined with the Christ event. As such, the recitation of Scripture and song cultivated an aural map of the cosmos re-created in Christ for the auditor. In the midst of a largely illiterate populace, Christianized rhetoric and chant had the power to reshape the sonic appetites and expectations of the general population.

The Christian tradition is therefore a sonic tradition. For all of the ambiguities and episodic suspicions toward music that we find throughout church history, Ralph Martin is certainly correct in saying: "The Christian Church was born in song."[5] Indeed, in what can be considered the first extant text depicting the Roman government's recognition of Christianity as a religion distinct from Judaism, Pliny the Younger's letter to the Emperor Trajan describes Christians in the early second century as those who assembled "on a set day before dawn and to sing a hymn among themselves to the Christ, as to a god."[6]

And so there is present throughout the history of Christian thought a sense that the redemption of the cosmos in Christ is revealed and thereby known through *music*, the ways in which Christianity *sounds*. Thus, rediscovering music in our time involves in many respects rediscovering our world and the ways in which we know.

4. MUSIC AS AURAL SACRAMENT

There is a particularly apropos scene that exemplifies this conception of music in the 1997 Italian film *Life Is Beautiful* (*La vita è bella*). The story revolves around an enthusiastic and charismatic Jewish man named Guido Orefice living in Nazi-occupied Europe. We meet Guido as he falls in love with a beautiful young woman named Dora. Guido pours all his humor and enthusiasm into courting her, greeting her every day in the market square with the words, "Good day, princess!" They eventually marry and are soon gifted with a baby boy whom they name Joshua. Guido loves Joshua with all his heart and pours the same enthusiastic humor and joy into the life of his son.

---

5. Ralph P. Martin, "Aspects of Worship in the New Testament Church," *Vox Evangelica II* (1963): 6–32.

6. For a further development of theology as essentially a *listening* act, see Bernd Wannenwetsch, " 'Take Heed What Ye Hear': Listening as a Moral, Transcendental and Sacramental Act," *Journal for the Royal Musical Association* 135, no. S1 (2010): 91–102.

  Chapter One. Life Is Beautiful: Music as Revelation

However, on the day of Joshua's fifth birthday, Guido's family is forced into a concentration camp. Guido and Joshua are both separated from Dora, as she is sequestered along with all the other women on the female side of the camp.

At one point in the movie, when Guido is assigned the duty of serving SS officers supper in the large house that overlooks the concentration camp, he gets a moment to himself and goes into a room that has a phonograph and records. He quickly sifts through the LPs and finds the song that he sang to Dora when he was courting her. He places the record on the turntable, points the shell-shaped speaker out the window, and the song proceeds to fill the evening sky. Dora hears the song from the other side of the camp. She stands and looks up; she realizes that Guido is still alive. At that very moment, as Guido gazes out of the window and she from far away looks up into the night sky, the echoes of music become for both of them what we might call an *aural sacrament*, a sonic bridge wherein they both become present in each other's lives.[7] Music provided a means of grace by which their hearts embraced each other in shared love and indescribable joy, as if they were both caught up on the wings of angels and lifted into Paradise itself.

We too can once again experience the presence of God, from which we were originally alienated, restored through the sacrament of sound. We can still hear the echoes, gaze at the refracted beauty, smell the fragrance, and taste the food of Paradise, for it is through Christ that the beauty of our heavenly Paradise, our original and future home, has been reawakened in this world. Sacred sound sanctifies our hearing to remind us that the darkness of this age is no match for the splendor of the world yet to come. The melodies of redemption thus bridge together two Advents, two heralding choirs of angels, preparing us and our world for their cosmic transfiguration.

---

7. For a development of Franz Liszt's musical theology, see Paul Barnes, "Franz Liszt and the Sacramental Bridge: Music as Theology of Presence," http://capress.link/eoe0101.

But to hear the eternity in these echoes, we're going to have to reorient ourselves not only to music, but also to the world itself. Such a reorientation begins with rediscovering the profound significance of sound for our human experience. We who are the "called ones," who receive "faith by hearing," are already somewhat privy to the significance of sound. However, few of us are fully aware of the manifold dimensionality of the acoustic world which, like my grandfather's garden, offers us a bouquet of audible fragrances and sonic delights that awaken our senses to a world unseen, an otherwise undisclosed reality, revealed to those with ears to hear. It is to that world that we now turn.

QUESTIONS FOR REFLECTION AND DISCUSSION

1. In what ways has music impacted your life?

2. Recall a moment when you heard a song for the first time in several years, only to remember people, places, and events you hadn't thought about for ages. What does that say about music and its capacity to communicate life experiences?

3. How have you noticed the "triumph of the visual" in our culture?

4. Do you think that our modern bias toward the visual has changed the way we perceive reality?

5. What would a "theology of listening" entail?

Suggested Listening Exercises

Listen to the first movement, "Kyrie Eleison," of J.S. Bach's *Mass in B Minor*. As you listen, reflect on how the music reveals the world in which Bach lived. Can you hear attributes and characteristics of the ideals of his culture? What does his music say about the nature of Christian worship? The order of the universe? The purpose of art? The ideals of community?

Now compare and contrast that with a highly modern piece such as *Philomel* by Milton Babbitt. What does this piece reveal about the world that Babbitt inhabits, and how does it contrast with the world of Bach?

You can reveal to your students that these two composers come from the same (Western) culture, two hundred years removed. Given the stark contrast between both worlds, you can then ask: What happened to our culture? What changed?

Suggestions for Further Reading

Paul Barnes, "Franz Liszt and the Sacramental Bridge: Music as Theology of Presence," http://capress.link/eoe0101.

Carol Harrison, *The Art of Listening in the Early Church* (Oxford: Oxford University Press, 2013).

David Hoews, ed., *The Varieties of Sensory Experience: A Sourcebook in the Anthropology of the Senses* (Toronto: University of Toronto Press, 1991).

CHAPTER TWO
Soundscapes: Making Sonic Sense

1. INTRODUCTION

In our last chapter, I introduced the classical notion of music as an aural sacrament, a sonic bridge by which the presence of another is experienced sonically by the listener. I think it's safe to say that we've all experienced this in some way. Each of us has heard a song, perhaps for the first time in many years, and suddenly, almost out of nowhere, people, places, and events which were previously absent from our recollections come to mind, often in extraordinary detail. Our hearts are stirred by perceptions, emotions, and inclinations that we haven't felt in quite some time, all of which were roused by a mere melody or simple tune.

What's going on here? Why is music such a powerful mode by which to communicate our past experiences of people, places, and events?

Acoustic space is a world of revelation.

One answer is found in the nature of sound itself. To understand the myriad ways in which music serves as a mode of wider human experience, we need to better appreciate the significance of the sonic dimension of our lives. In this chapter, we'll discover the profound world of acoustic space, and the several ways in which soundscapes shape our experience of ourselves and of our world.

2. The World of Sound

I quoted previously the insight from theologian John Hull that sound is a world of revelation. I want to expand on that observation. Hull's book on his experience of going blind, *Touching the Rock*, provides for us a profound starting point of discovering how sound shapes our encounter with the world around us. Hull writes:

> What is the world of sound? I have been spending some time outdoors trying to respond to the special nature of the acoustic world . . . the tangible world sets up only as many points of reality as can be touched by the body, and this seems to be restricted to one problem at a time. I can explore the splinters on the park bench with the tip of my finger but I cannot, at the same time, concentrate upon exploring the pebbles with my big toe. . . . The world revealed by sound is so different. . . . On Holy Saturday I sat in Cannon Hill Park while the children were playing. . . . The footsteps came from both sides. They met, mingled, separated again. From the next bench, there was the rustle of a newspaper and the murmur of conversation. . . . I heard the steady, deep roar of the traffic, the buses and the trucks. . . . [The acoustic world] stays the same whichever way I turn my head. This is not true of the perceptible [i.e., visually perceptible] world. It changes as I turn my head. New things come into view. The view looking that way is quite different from the view looking this way. It is not like that with sound. . . . This is a world which I cannot shut out, which goes on all around me, and which gets on with its own life. . . . Acoustic space is a world of revelation.[1]

I find that Hull's analysis of acoustic space captures profoundly the uniqueness of sound for our human experience. Roger Scruton observes that sound is irreducibly abstract in that it's not attached

---

1. Hull, *Touching the Rock*, 61–64; as cited in Begbie, *Theology, Music and Time*, 24–25.

Chapter Two. Soundscapes: Making Sonic Sense

as an attribute or quality of things, like color.[2] Sound in fact can be heard without knowing the source or the object producing the sound. By contrast, I can't experience the color green without experiencing the object to which such color is attributed. Similar to Hull, Jeremy Begbie expands on this observation by noting that while discrete objects can only be in one place at one time, sound can surround us and envelop us.[3] My experience of the world through sight is inescapably *directional*: I can see only what is in front of me. However, my experience of sound is *omnidirectional*: I can hear all around me, above and below. Don Ihde observes: "I may hear all around me, or, as a field-shape, sound *surrounds* me in my embodied positionality."[4] Moreover, while I can't see what is going on in the room next to the one that I occupy, I can hear its activities; sound increases exponentially my field of perception, which has fascinating applications to music that we shall develop in the chapters that follow.[5]

3. The Visible Invisible and the Hearing Body

There are two aspects of the above observations that I think crucial for understanding the nature of sound and its relation to our humanity.

First, *sound makes visible the invisible*. A fascinating dimension of sound is that it alerts us to that which we cannot account for in any particular object or thing. Even the frequencies that make up sound cannot themselves, at a phenomenological level, account for what

---

2. See Scruton's full discussion on the nature of sound in *The Aesthetics of Music* (Oxford: Clarendon Press, 1997), 1–18.
3. Begbie, *Theology, Music and Time*, 24.
4. Don Ihde, *Listening and Voice: Phenomenologies of Sound* (Albany: State University of New York Press, 2007), 74.
5. "In short," Begbie (*Theology, Music and Time*, 24), notes, "there appears to be the attribute of 'omnipresence' in music."

sound actually is.[6] Jean-Luc Nancy puts it this way: while I can hear what I see, I can never see what I hear.[7] Here's an example I like to give to my students. Imagine sitting in a movie theater and watching an epic battle scene from Peter Jackson's depiction of the Tolkien trilogy, *The Lord of the Rings*. What kind of sounds would you be hearing? Certainly we would hear loud dramatic music, the clashing of steel swords, battle cries, and the like. Now imagine that something goes wrong with the sound system and the speakers go completely silent. The movie continues to play, but there is no sound. Has anything in any way changed visually? The answer of course is no; the *visual* aspect of the film experience goes on unaffected. What disappeared from our experience is a profound sonic dimension *that cannot be seen*; the soundtrack is, in a word, *invisible*. Thus, one of the mystical elements of sound is that it makes the invisible "visible" or sensed.

Secondly, *sound is "heard" by the whole body*. We encounter sounds not merely through our ears; rather, sound permeates our entire bodies. Ihde draws out the implications of hearing for our embodiment: "Phenomenologically I do not merely hear with my *ears*, I *hear* with my whole body. My ears are at best the *focal* organs of hearing. This may be detected quite dramatically in listening to loud rock music. The bass notes reverberate in my stomach, and even my feet 'hear' the sound of the auditory orgy."[8] Here, I can't help but think of the unfortunate times I've stopped at a red light next to a low-riding car with a woofer the size of an army tank, blaring bass-heavy beats that rattle my car windows, not to mention the loose change in my cupholder. In fact, in a manner similar to the vibrating eardrum, this is why we dance; dance is simply one of the ways in which the whole body hears; in other words, a dancing body is a hearing body.

---

6. It's tempting to think here of the riddle as to whether a tree falling in the forest still makes a sound if there were no one to hear it.

7. Jean-Luc Nancy, *Listening*, trans. Charlotte Mandell (New York: Fordham University Press, 2007), 10.

8. Ihde, *Listening and Voice*, 45.

 Chapter Two. Soundscapes: Making Sonic Sense

4. Encountering the World of Sounds

So, *what* in fact are we hearing? What are these sound waves and frequencies communicating to us and how do we make sense of them? How does acoustic space shape our perception of the world around us? In what follows, I list several ways in which sound shapes our human experience. Note that I offer here a representative rather than an exhaustive list; your classroom discussions may reveal many more!

a. Time

Our perception of time is often inextricably linked to sounds. Perhaps the most obvious example is the alarm or the tick per second from an analog clock or watch, or the church bells ringing on the hour. We can also hear time in terms of duration, like the extended and continuous sound of a fan blowing or a motor running. Morning can be identified with the sounds of birds tweeting, while evening is characterized by the chirping of crickets. Even the seasons can be heard. Nighttime in a spring forest finds a symphony of chitters and cheeps, while a winter evening is cool, calm, and still; the sounds of the beach suggest summer, and the crunch of leaves underfoot indicates fall. Even cultural celebrations of time can be heard, as is the case every December in the West. In short, "sound embodies the sense of time."[9]

b. Space

Musicians are particularly sensitive to the sound of space. The sound check is usually the first thing musicians do when entering a concert venue, determining the quality of sound in the performance hall. The extent to which sound echoes as well as the nuances of timbre and tone indicate such features as the space's size and shape. The materiality of ceilings, walls, and floors, made up of wood, plaster, glass, or stone, all affect in some way a space's acoustic dimension-

---

9. Ihde, *Listening and Voice*, 84.

ality. We can also hear the difference between inside and outside, a small space and a large space, a pub and a daycare, an indoor pool and an outdoor pool. The space inside a car sounds different from the space in an auditorium.

c. Region

As we extend the concept of space, we encounter the acoustic dimensions of regions. Here we encounter distinct accents associated with different nations or cultures; often a person's home province or territory can be detected by their inflection of speech, such as in the American South. We can tell the difference audibly between urban regions, characterized by inflated activity and decibel, and rural regions. The Middle East is sonically distinguished by the sound of the *Adhan*, or call to prayer, echoing from towering minarets, while Japan is recognized by the plaintive plucking sounds of the koto.

d. Shapes, surfaces, and interiors

We might be surprised that, upon reflection, shapes have sounds. If I were to put a marble in a shoebox, the sound it would make as I tilt the box would be markedly different than the sound of a die or some other cube. The sound of a basketball or bowling ball rolling on a hard court is quite different from the sound made on the same surface by a skipping football or shuttlecock. The hard court itself evidences the fact that we can hear surfaces: the squeak of the basketball sneakers is remarkably different from the sound of tennis shoes on a clay court; the sound of high heels walking on wooden floors is rather different than on gravel. So too the creak of the wooden floor and the muffling of the rug. And even interiors exemplify sonic significance, such as when knocking on walls "looking" for a stud or stringer into which to drive a nail to hang a picture. And in terms of making the invisible visible, we often get the first sight of our new baby while inside the mother's womb through a technology termed *ultrasound.*

    Chapter Two. Soundscapes: Making Sonic Sense

e. Directionality

We noted previously that sound is omnidirectional; it transcends the discrete specificity of visual encounters in the world around us. Along with this, sound is able to communicate proximity in its own unique way. Don Ihde cites the work of Georg von Békésy, who has shown that our sense of directionality is much more precise with sharp clicking sounds than with tones. This is perhaps why we intuitively snap our fingers, pound a desk, or speak more sharply when trying to get someone's attention.[10] Moreover, most of us are aware of something called the Doppler effect, which involves either the increase or decrease of sound waves as they move closer to or father from the perceiver. Faint sounds are intuitively sensed as distant and far away, whereas increasingly loud and obtrusive sounds are appropriated as approaching and immanent.

f. Size

Another dimension of sound perception involves size. Perhaps you remember the scene from the movie *Jurassic Park*, when the stranded tourist played by Jeff Goldblum hears the approaching footsteps of the massive tyrannosaurus rex, the low thud echoing throughout the shaking earth. The power of the scene is in what is merely heard and not seen: the colossal size of an approaching threat. Contrast this with the sound of a toddler's footsteps pattering across the family room floor. We can distinguish the size difference in children's and adults' steps and movements, and even from the depth and range of voice. We make sonic distinctions between an immense Mack truck and a midsized Honda Civic.

g. Emotion

It perhaps goes without saying that different emotions entail different sounds. Laughter, cheering, chuckling, and giggling are all

---

10. Ihde, *Listening and Voice*, 75.

associated with happiness and enjoyment, while crying, groaning, and whimpering are associated with sorrow and disappointment. A scream can either be an indicator of fear or elation depending on its timbre and character. In sporting events, we can hear how the game is going based on the reactions of the fans: victory is signified by cheers reaching upward while defeat is accompanied by groans falling downward. And how many of us have been told: "It's not what you said, but *how* you said it that concerns me."

5. AUDITORY FIELDS AND THE NUMINOUS

The combination of these variegated sounds in our sonic experience of life creates what Ihde terms an "auditory field," which involves the human brain's perception of focal or foregrounded sounds and fringe or background sounds. The multidimensionality of sounds creates in effect a soundscape, an acoustic context in which I am sonically absorbed. The most distant sound available to the ear represents the frontier or border of the soundscape, followed by gradations of sonic proximity to the listener, all orchestrated coherently by the human mind.

The fact that such an auditory field is itself nondiscrete, revelatory of an invisible and intangible dimension of reality, has had a profound impact on the formation of our humanity. Most profoundly, soundscapes have contributed to the experience of the supernatural, or what the German theologian Rudolf Otto terms the "numinous": the nondiscursive, ineffable experience of the holy or divine.[11] The numinous is "the emotion of a creature, submerged and overwhelmed by its own nothingness in contrast to that which is supreme above all creatures. . . . [The feeling expresses] the note

---

11. Rudolf Otto, *The Idea of the Holy*, trans. John W. Harvey (Oxford: Oxford University Press, 1950), 5–11.

Chapter Two. Soundscapes: Making Sonic Sense

of submergence into nothingness before an overpowering, absolute might of some kind. . . . The numinous is thus felt as objective and outside the self."[12] According to Otto, the object of the numinous is expressed as *mysterium tremendum*, that which is "quite beyond the sphere of the usual, the intelligible, and the familiar," characterized by "awefulness," "overpoweringness," and "energy," the encounter of which evokes variegated and complex emotional reactions, ranging from the terrifying to the sublime.[13]

> *The acoustic dimensions of space and time,*
> *direction and surface, size and shape,*
> *reveal to us a world that transcends*
> *our sight, one that surrounds us*
> *and yet in a very real way eludes us.*

According to Otto, one of the primary means by which one encounters the numinous is through sound, both in terms of heard sounds as well as uttered sounds. He cites as an example the Hindu employment of the holy syllable *Om* (or *Aum*) as a meditation mantra. Noting its lack of semiotic or referential specificity, Otto writes: "It is really simply a sort of growl or groan, sounding up from within as the quasi-reflex expression of profound emotion in circumstances of a numinous-magical nature, and serving to relieve consciousness of a felt burden, almost physical in its constraining force."[14] Otto's observations corroborate those of nineteenth-century musicologist Edmund Gurney:

> The link between sound and the supernatural is
> profound and widespread. . . . Possibly sound—like
> the gods a powerful unseen presence—is an unac-
> knowledged model for our concept of the other-

---

12. Otto, *Holy*, 10–11.
13. Otto, *Holy*, 12–26.
14. Otto, *Holy*, 197.

worldly. . . . Ritual sound makes the transcendent immanent."[15]

6. SUMMARY

Our world is a deeply sonic world. The acoustic dimensions of space and time, direction and surface, size and shape, reveal to us a world that transcends our sight, one that surrounds us and yet in a very real way eludes us. But what of those sounds that transfigure into melody, harmony, and rhythm? What kind of sonic world does song reveal to us? As Scruton writes:

> The sound world is inherently other, and other in an interesting way: it is not just that we do not belong in it; it is that we *could* not belong in it: it is metaphysically apart from us. And yet we have a complete view of it, and discover in it, through music, the very life that is ours. *There* lies the mystery, or part of it.[16]

It is to that mystery that we now turn.

QUESTIONS FOR REFLECTION AND DISCUSSION

1. What are the ways in which sounds are different from what we see?

2. What are some examples of sound making the invisible visible?

3. What are ways in which the whole body "hears"?

4. What are some ways in which we hear time?

---

15. Cited in Guy L. Beck, ed., *Sacred Sound: Experiencing Music in World Religions* (Waterloo, Ontario: Wilfred Laurier University Press, 2006), 22–23.
16. Scruton, *Aesthetics*, 13–14.

    Chapter Two. Soundscapes: Making Sonic Sense

5. Take a moment to listen to your immediate surroundings. What's the farthest sound you can hear? Can you hear sounds above and below you? Is there an arrangement of sounds in terms of proximity?

6. How do different spaces exemplify different sounds?

7. Can you guess where a person is from by how she or he speaks? In what ways?

8. Think of ways in which you can hear different emotions. What are the differences between a laugh of joy and a shriek of horror?

SUGGESTED LISTENING EXERCISE

In two to three pages, write about a sonic experience of your choice. This may involve sitting in an artificial environment (home, café, or coffeehouse) or in a natural environment (forest, hillside, beach). Record observations of the multitude of sounds around you and think through how the convergence of these sounds impacts the way you experience and perceive the world in terms of time, space, directionality, emotion, etc.

SUGGESTIONS FOR FURTHER READING

Don Ihde, *Listening and Voice: Phenomenologies of Sound* (Albany: State University of New York Press, 2007).

Mark Johnson, *The Meaning of the Body: Aesthetics of Human Understanding* (Chicago: University of Chicago Press, 2012).

Jean-Luc Nancy, *Listening*, trans. Charlotte Mandell (New York: Fordham University Press, 2007).

Jonathan Rée, *I See a Voice: A Philosophical History of Language, Deafness and the Senses* (New York: HarperCollins, 1999).

Part II
Echoes of Eternity

CHAPTER THREE
What Is Music? Exploring the World of Song

1. INTRODUCTION

I expressed earlier my concern that we in the modern age have lost the profoundly mystical sense of music, which was once highly formative in shaping and cultivating our humanity. To the end of rediscovering that mystical and formative power, we rehearsed the *revelatory* significance of sound itself. The sonic world discloses to us a world unseen; we might say it makes visible the invisible. Acoustic space surrounds and overwhelms us with temporal and spatial dimensionality otherwise impervious to our sight, such that there is little to justify our Enlightenment-inspired visualism so prone to marginalizing the auditory to the background.

With this in mind, I want to take us further into the revelatory world of sound in the guise of music itself. We'll begin by offering a definition or description of music, what accounts for its meaning, and then explore eight biblical and cross-cultural features of music identified by ethnomusicologists. In so doing, we'll find that music both utilizes and transfigures the various ways in which acoustic environments shape our experience of the world, and discover how the revelatory nature of music is able to comparably cultivate bodies and souls, societies and communities, in Scripture as well as in the various musical traditions across the globe.

2. Defining Music

In his work *The History of Music Aesthetics*, Enrico Fubini begins his study with what he considers the elusive, ineffable, even mystical nature of music:

> Since ancient times, philosophers, intellectuals and musicians have written about music and have clearly believed it to have a particular status among the arts, being endowed with special powers. . . . Both the fascination it has always exerted and its extreme elusiveness are due primarily to the nature of its expressiveness: it expresses something, and yet, despite the complexity of its "language," it says nothing definite about anything; while everybody, even the strictest of formalist thinkers, seems to concur in ascribing to music a certain power of expression nobody has yet succeeded in defining clearly what it is that music expresses or how it does so.[1]

Fubini's observations should attune us to the reductionist risk inherent in any attempt to define and delineate the phenomenon of music. As the maxim "music begins where words end" entails, music is a mystery that evades verbal precision.

Nonetheless, our engagements with music evoke the need to somehow articulate what it is we are encountering. In his excellent study, theologian and musician Jeremy Begbie offers what I believe to be a most helpful definition or description of music. While recognizing that the word *music* speaks of a huge range of phenomena, Begbie argues that all music can be understood as temporally organized patterns of pitched sounds or tones both made and perceived.[2] In what follows, I want to unpack this definition, leaving the issue of music's temporality for development below.

---

1. Enrico Fubini, *The History of Music Aesthetics* (London: Macmillan, 1990), xi–xii.
2. Begbie, *Theology, Music and Time*, 9.

 Chapter Three. What Is Music? Exploring the World of Song

As we explored in our previous chapter, the most basic component of music is *sound*. Sounds are comprised of *pitch*, which involves the frequency or rate of vibration in a sound wave; the higher or lower the frequency, the higher or lower the pitch.[3] However, with music, sound and pitch transfigure into *tone*, a term generally used to denote any discrete pitched sound that is recognized as musical.[4] Tone involves a deliberate intentional inflection of pitch for musical or communicative effect, as with the complaint: "I don't like your tone." Tones in turn are arranged to comprise a *melody*, which is constituted by (1) a *range* of lowest to highest notes, (2) a *direction* of ascending or descending notes, and (3) a *character* or *quality* evoked by the interplay between the range and direction.[5] The overlapping resonance of the tones within the melodic contour creates a *harmony*, which involves the simultaneous sounding of two or more tones.

Of further interest in Begbie's definition of music is what he sees as the reciprocal dimension of music making and music perceiving. Music making occurs when someone transforms sounds into tones, while music perceiving occurs when such a transformation is heard and received as such. That music involves *both* music making *and* music perceiving means that there is an irreducibly *communal* nature to music, which we shall explore in further detail below.

3. MEANING AND MUSIC

There are two schools of thought that account for the meaning that we associate with music, which involves the "purpose" or "intention" of music: its expressiveness and gesture. On the one hand, there are what are called *extrinsic* theories of music meaning

---

3. Michael B. Bakan, *World Music: Traditions and Transformations* (New York: McGraw-Hill, 2007), 43.
4. Begbie, *Theology, Music and Time*, 9n2.
5. Bakan, *World Music*, 44.

and, on the other, *intrinsic* theories of music meaning.[6] Extrinsic theories locate music meaning in things other than music; the expressive effects of music are the result of associations we make that are external to the musical event. In this sense, music has the capacity to relate in some manner to some extramusical/nonmusical object or objects' states of affairs. Sad music has a way of relating to sorrowful feelings, or happy music has a way of relating to our joyful experiences, and thus we associate those experiences with music. Intrinsic theories, on the other hand, stress the relationships between the constituent elements of music itself. I wouldn't be relating a piece of music to an emotion or to an event apart from the fact that the notes in the piece have an inherent relationship or form that does in fact capture that emotion or event.

In many respects, the intrinsic and extrinsic conceptions of musical meaning and expression are really two different sides of the same coin. Considered in and of themselves, each theory is inescapably reductionist. Instead, I would see the two theories coming together in what Christopher Small calls "musicking," which refers to the interrelationship of all the aspects of musical performance.[7] In order for music to work *as music*, it must cohere both intrinsically and extrinsically; music involves not merely the relationships between notes and chords, rhythm and meter, but also between the people who are making and listening to the music, and even the society and its natural resources. Small writes:

> They [relationships] are to be found not only between
> those organized sounds which are conventionally
> thought of as being the stuff of musical meaning but
> also between the people who are taking part, in what-
> ever capacity, in the performance; and they model, or
> stand as metaphor for, ideal relationships as the partici-
> pants in the performance imagine them to be: relation-

6. Begbie, *Theology, Music and Time*, 11; Bakan, *World Music*, 11.
7. Christopher Small, *Musicking: The Meanings of Performing and Listening* (Middletown, CT: Wesleyan University Press, 1998), 9.

ships between person and person, between individual
and society, between humanity and the natural world
and even perhaps the supernatural world.[8]

Thus, in the act of musicking, the extrinsic and intrinsic qualities
of music become one.

4. The Features of Music: Revelation of Sonic Worlds

In the previous chapter, we explored several ways in which acoustic environments shape our experience of the world, revealing to us unseen dimensions of life and reality. This capacity for disclosing the invisible renders soundscapes highly effective in communicating the unseen presence of the supernatural, which, as we'll see in this chapter, is exemplified by the sonic features of rituals throughout world cultures. I concluded our survey by asking the question: What of those sounds that transfigure into melody, harmony, and rhythm? What kind of sonic world does song reveal to us? In what follows, I want us to explore *eight features* of music that complement the number of ways in which acoustic environments shape our life experiences. In so doing, we will draw from examples in Scripture as well as from a number of musical cultures from around the world to demonstrate the transcultural commonality of such features.[9] By exploring these characteristics of music making and perceiving, we can account not only for music's revelatory significance, but also for its formative power in shaping our minds and bodies into distinctive visions of humanity.

a. Music is performed.

The first feature of music involves the fact that music is in some way performed. Of significance for musical performance is the unique

---

8. Small, *Musicking*, 13. Small's reference to theological uncertainty ("perhaps the supernatural world") betrays his unfortunate secularism.
9. We'll be developing the distinctively Christian use of these features in the chapters that follow.

way in which otherwise disparate things are brought together into a conceptual and experiential whole. What performance theorists have observed is that performances have the peculiar power to *generate* or *create* distinctive realities; performances construct their own unique states of affairs by which life is experienced anew.[10] For example, as a classical guitarist, I travel to a concert venue with my guitar in its case and musical scores in my briefcase. In that instance, the guitar, the musical score, and I are all distinct and disparate. Yet when I walk onto the concert stage and sit down to play, in that moment, the guitar, music, and I become *one*; we are completely inseparable. Through the performance of music, otherwise disparate things transfigure into a composite whole. This includes, of course, the place and audience as well, such that no two performances are the same.

As an act of performance, then, music has the power to enact distinct visions of the cosmos, revealing the relationship between diverse particulars and their unifying whole. For example, Scripture depicts the music of the temple as manifesting the very presence of God. Upon the finishing of Solomon's temple, the Levitical choir praised and thanked the Lord "with one voice," and then the glory of the Lord filled the temple (2 Chron. 5:11-14). The connection between music and the presence of God may be found in the Hebrew term for "praise," *hll*, which also means "shine."[11] The music of the Levitical choir thus invoked the radiance of the presence of the God who created heaven and earth, thereby designating the temple and its city, Jerusalem, as the center of the universe, the city of God.

The performance of music serves a comparable cosmic significance in the enchanting world of Buddhism. In writing about Buddhist practices of music, Sean Williams notes:

---

10. Klaus-Peter Köpping, Bernhard Leistle, and Michael Rudolph, eds., *Ritual and Identity: Performative Practices as Effective Transformations of Social Reality* (Berlin: Lit Verlag, 2006), 17.
11. Margaret Barker, *Temple Themes in Christian Worship* (London: T&T Clark International, 2007), 142.

          Chapter Three. What Is Music? Exploring the World of Song

It is in Mahāyāna Buddhism that sacred sound in performance is fully realized, and where the cosmological significance of Buddhism is physically enacted through musical concepts and behaviors. Whether it appears in the highlighting of silence and emptiness through the sounds of a bamboo flute in Japan or in the constantly moving progression of sound through time as a reminder of life's impermanence, Buddhist music represents an enactment of Buddhist ideals and practices.[12]

The important point here is that a Buddhist cosmology, its sense of transience and impermanence, is most effectively expressed and realized in musical performance.

b. Music is iconic.

The second feature of music involves its iconicity; that is, music tends to actually resemble or embody what it seeks to communicate or express. In this sense, music is quite different from language. For example, I am perfectly capable of talking intelligibly about sadness without personally experiencing sad emotions while speaking. Conversely, I can lecture on the importance of happiness while being personally depressed. This is because words are technically *symbols*, and in the field of semiotics (the study of signs), symbols communicate their referent through a cultural correspondence between the sign and the thing signified. A canine could be symbolized as *dog* by English speakers, *inu* by Japanese speakers, and *Hund* by Germans. There is no necessary or transcultural connection between a symbol and what it signifies. However, music is very different from words; music cannot communicate an emotion or gesture intelligibly without actually *resembling* that emotion or gesture. Music cannot express sadness without itself being sad, or happiness without melodies, harmonies, and rhythms that exemplify the gestures we associate with happiness. This is music's iconicity; icons

---

12. Sean Williams, "Buddhism and Music," in Beck, *Sacred Sound*, 187.

communicate their referent through a resemblance or similarity to the thing signified.[13]

We can perceive the iconicity of music in Scripture by contrasting the different uses of instruments in two different scenarios. First, notice how the blowing of the trumpet at Sinai complements the sounds of thunder along with the visuals of lightning and smoke surrounding the holy mountain: "Now when all the people saw the thunder and the flashes of lightning and the sound of the trumpet and the mountain smoking, the people were afraid and trembled" (Exod. 20:18). By contrast, we are told that when David played his lyre for Saul, the king "was refreshed and was well, and the harmful spirit departed from him" (1 Sam. 16:23). The volume and dynamics of wind instruments can produce an almost ear-shattering reaction, while the fragility of the stringed lyre evokes a comparably gentle response. Imagine switching the instruments while trying to maintain the original effects!

Program music most particularly exploits the iconic nature of music. The symphonic poem entitled *The Moldau* by the Bohemian composer Bedřich Smetana portrays profoundly the flow of water in the Vltava River in his native Czech countryside. Film scores also utilize music's iconicity. Think of the difference between the kind of soundtrack associated with a horror film such as *Friday the 13th* and Disney's *Aladdin*. Their respective film scores express sonically the particular ethos associated with each movie—so much so that switching soundtracks would lead to aesthetic incoherence!

Sonic iconicity enables music to express even the imperceptible. In African music, the foundational drumbeat often mimics what is considered the pulse or heartbeat of the cosmos, which emerges from the ground through the drum and to the listener's ear. The Tuvan practice of throat singing, where overtones are heard over a

---

13. For a development of music's iconicity in relation to language, see Begbie, *Theology, Music and Time*, 20–23; cf. Scruton, *Aesthetics*, 344.

    Chapter Three. What Is Music? Exploring the World of Song

bass tone, images the animistic spiritual presence within the natural sounds of gurgling water and swishing wind.[14] And Islamic chant recites the message of Allah, who cannot be seen or heard, to his faithful, making the inaudible audible.[15]

c. Music is temporal.

As Begbie's definition/description above indicates, music is inherently *temporal*.[16] Musical temporality is principally manifested through the means of *rhythm*. Rhythm is comprised of beats, which involves the duration between tones, and beats are in turn systematically grouped into a meter or time signature, which gives the song its groove or pulse, what we tap our feet to. While rhythm refers to the various durations given to a sequence of tones, meter configures beats into an overall musical pulse by emphasizing some beats and de-emphasizing others, creating a wavelike pattern of rhythm. As Begbie notes: "Rhythmic patterns . . . 'ride' the metrical waves, and in so doing, reveal the shape of the waves."[17] The shape of meter involves a movement from one strong beat to the next, creating a sense of movement toward and anticipation of the next emphasized beat.

The rhythmic temporality of music reflects the "evening and morning" rhythm inherent in the order of creation. Throughout the biblical narrative, the life of Israel is structured according to this daily rhythm of dawn and dusk. Two sacrifices of lambs were to be offered, one in the morning and the other in the evening (Exod. 29:38-43; cf. Num. 28:3-8; Ezra 3:3). In Exodus 30:7-9, the lamps in the sanctuary were to be adjusted and incense offered on the altar every morning and evening. Malachi 1:11 prophesies a worldwide worship in these temporal terms: "For from the rising of the sun to

14. Theodore C. Levin and Michael E. Edgerton, "The Throat Singers of Tuva," *Scientific American* (Sept. 1999): 80.
15. Regula Qureshi, "Islam and Music," in Beck, *Sacred Sound*, 89.
16. For an overview of the philosophical issues related to time, see Begbie, *Theology, Music and Time*, 29–33.
17. Begbie, *Theology, Music and Time*, 41.

its setting my name will be great among the nations, and in every place incense will be offered to my name, and a pure offering. For my name will be great among the nations, says the LORD of hosts." Hence, God calls Israel to teach the law of God to their children "when you lie down, and when you rise" (Deut. 6:7).

Perhaps no other feature of African music is as prominent as its emphasis on rhythm. African scholars have observed that rhythm is interpreted as a bridge between life and death, between being and nothingness, between time and eternity.[18] The drum sounds forth the pulse of the cosmos, which can in turn be entered into through a music and dance that conforms individuals and the community to this cosmic rhythmic flow. Similarly, Tibetan Buddhist chant employs rhythmic formulas that organize beats around sacred words. The performance practice involves monks sitting in rows facing one another while a leader, known as *dbu mdzad*, leads the singing with percussion.[19] This temporality intrinsic to music extends to marking particular conceptions of time. There are, for example, Indian *ragas* that are associated with different times of the day and the different sentiments or moods associated with those times. Christian and Jewish music traditions are notable for the ways in which the calendar is punctuated by song, as with Advent and Christmas for the former and Yom Kippur for the latter.

d. Music is communal.

Because music involves the interaction between music making and music hearing, it is irreducibly communal in nature. It perhaps goes without saying that virtually every culture or social movement is characterized by its songs. This is because music is so often the microcosmic embodiment of social order. For example, congregational singing is prominent throughout Scripture. David declared:

18. E. Elochukwu Uzukwu, *Worship as Body Language: Introduction to Christian Worship: An African Orientation* (Collegeville, MN: The Liturgical Press, 1997), 12.
19. Williams, "Buddhism and Music," 180.

"I will tell of your name to my brothers; in the midst of the congregation I will praise you" (Ps. 22:22; cf. Heb. 2:12). Jesus and his disciples sang a hymn together following the Last Supper (Matt. 26:30), and in the book of Revelation we read of all of heaven singing together in praise of God (cf. Rev. 5:9-14; 14:3).

The ancient Greeks considered music to be a key process of socialization. Not only did the students participate in regular public music competitions, but the ordered chorus and the tuning of the strings of the lyre were paradigmatic for the harmonious and well-governed city. Indeed, Aristotle went so far as to argue that the state cannot exist without a well-trained chorus.[20]

In African traditions, music serves to unite one with not only the wider community, but also "the vast play of forces that encompass and connect all beings."[21] In his discussion of Andaman Island dancing, anthropologist Alfred Radcliffe-Brown observes:

> As the dancer loses himself in the dance, as he becomes
> absorbed in the unified community, he reaches a state
> of elation in which he feels himself filled with an
> energy beyond his ordinary state . . . at the same time
> finding himself in complete and ecstatic harmony with
> all the fellow members of his community.[22]

In Buddhist music, the individual self is lost in the *Saṅgha*, or community, which serves to resolve the problem of attaching importance to one's own voice. "Group chanting," writes Sean Williams, "mostly in unison, causes the self to become absorbed into the community."[23] And in Sufism, musically inspired assemblies are central to their ritual practices. Devotees gather together as an "assembly of listening," or *samā*, to hear and sing mystical poetry and hymns,

---

20. Aristotle, *Politics* 1325b37–8.
21. Richard Hodges, "Drum Is the Ear of God: Africa's Inner World of Music," http://capress.link/eoe0301.
22. Cited in Roy A. Rappaport, *Ritual and Religion in the Making of Humanity* (Cambridge: Cambridge University Press, 1999), 226.
23. Williams, "Buddhism and Music," 186.

replete with all manner of instrumentation, culminating corporately in an ecstatic encounter with God.[24]

Music resists specificity and transcends instantiation; rather, music is the emotion that it is expressing. Sad music does not depict a sad event; rather, sad music depicts the essence of sadness.

The communal nature of music accounts for why virtually every political or social movement and culture is expressed in corporate song. When we sing together, we are not merely claiming to create a social harmony and unity, we are *demonstrating* social harmony. Our collective singing realizes and manifests tangibly in time and space the very unity our communities and social movements profess. Music is the ideal community in microcosm.

e. Music is emotional.

It has long been recognized that music has very strong connections with our emotional life. The perception of music is not merely for the mind but also for the heart, the soul, and thus enables us to experience our humanity in profoundly moving ways. It was the nineteenth-century German philosopher Arthur Schopenhauer who had a profound insight on the relationship between music and emotion. He wrote:

> (Music) never expresses the phenomenon, but only the inner nature, the in-itself, of every phenomenon, the will itself. Therefore music does not express this or that particular and definite pleasure, this or that affliction, pain, sorrow, horror, gaiety, merriment, or peace of mind, but joy, pain, sorrow, horror, gaiety, merriment, peace of mind *themselves*, to a certain extent in the

---

24. Qureshi, "Islam and Music," 98.

 Chapter Three. What Is Music? Exploring the World of Song

abstract, their essential nature, without any accessories,
and so also without the motives for them.[25]

What Schopenhauer is saying here is that unlike the other arts, music communicates human emotion irrespective of discrete persons, places, or events. If I want to communicate the emotion of sadness through, say, a painting or poem, the only way I can do so is to paint or write about an *instantiation* of sadness, portraying a specific circumstance of the particular emotion that I am seeking to express. However, music resists specificity and transcends instantiation; rather, music *is* the emotion that it is expressing. Sad music does not depict a sad event; rather, sad music depicts the *essence* of sadness.

The Apostle Paul drew from this logic between music and emotion or, perhaps better, emotion *in* music, when he exhorted the Ephesians to be "filled with the Spirit, addressing one another in psalms and hymns and spiritual songs, singing and making melody to the Lord with your heart, giving thanks always and for everything to God the Father in the name of our Lord Jesus Christ" (Eph. 5:18-20). James tells us: "Is anyone among you suffering? Let him pray. Is anyone cheerful? Let him sing praise" (5:13). Note how James linked together the act of singing (*psalletō*) with a cheerful or merry emotion. James appears to be echoing Psalm 95:1-2:

> Oh come, let us sing to the Lord;
>> let us make a joyful noise to the rock of our salvation!
> Let us come into his presence with thanksgiving;
>> let us make a joyful noise to him with songs of praise!

Notice too the difference in emotional effect between the blowing of the trumpet for the people at Sinai and David's playing of the lyre for the troubled soul of Saul that we looked at above. In Exodus, the people trembled at the sound of trumpet and thunder, while Saul was soothed by the sounds of the lyre (Exod. 20:18; 1 Sam. 16:23).

---

25. Arthur Schopenhauer, *The World as Will and Representation*, Vol. 1, trans. E.F.J. Payne (Indian Hills, CO: Falcon's Wing Press, 1958), 261.

A comparable contrast between music and emotion is evident in Christ's denunciation of Israel's hypocrisy: "We played the flute for you, and you did not dance; we sang a dirge, and you did not mourn" (Matt. 11:17). Again, note the logic between the type of music and its corresponding emotional effect.

Now this extraordinary emotional significance of music, according to Walter Ong, is part of how sound is able to convey a sense of presence more than the tactile of the visual senses. "Since sound expresses the interiority of people more than other sense experience, including movement and gesture, it best serves to bind people together."[26] In fact, David Burrows argues that this emotional capacity of music is deeper than language, and thus it is the tonal dimension of sound, as opposed to speaking, that more fully unites people instead of dividing them.[27]

f. Music is physical.

Musical practice is inescapably *embodied*. Begbie notes: "Our own physical, physiological and neurological make-up mediates and shapes the production and experience of sound to a very high degree."[28] Not only is the body actively engaged in music making, but also in music perceiving. Perhaps nowhere is this reciprocity more evident than in dance. After the people of God were rescued from Egypt, we are told that Miriam, Aaron's sister, "took a tambourine in her hand, and all the women went out after her with tambourines and dancing" (Exod. 15:20). David, too, in bringing the Ark of the Covenant to Jerusalem, led the procession in by dancing (2 Sam. 6:14).

African dance in particular is exceptional in its distinctively *pantomimic* use of the body. Because the body is envisioned as a microcosmic replication of the macrocosmic universe, the pulse of which resounds through the beat of the drum, African dance involves

---

26. Beck, *Sacred Sound*, 11.
27. Cited in Beck, *Sacred Sound*, 11.
28. Begbie, *Theology, Music and Time*, 15.

     Chapter Three. What Is Music? Exploring the World of Song

moving all parts of the body in imitation of the created world. Dancers embody everything from heroic virtue postures to flames of fire, from stomping elephants to crawling insects, from fluctuating rivers to the flight of birds.[29]

Another example is the Sufi practice of whirling, which mimics the counterclockwise movement of the cosmos to create a harmonious relationship with God. It is through whirling that the body can be transcended and the soul reaches what is considered a more primordial state, where Love is the only existing force, thus enabling whirlers to experience the essence of their existence.[30] And in the Cuban synchronistic religion known as Santería or Orisha, the musical body of the worshipper becomes a receptacle of spirits and divine communion.[31]

g. Music is ecological.

Music making and hearing arise from an engagement with the distinctive configurations of the physical world we inhabit. Thus, the kinds of instruments that are played are often transformations of the natural resources available to a culture. Take, for example, the instruments resounding in Psalm 150:3-6:

> Praise him with trumpet sound;
>   praise him with lute and harp!
> Praise him with tambourine and dance;
>   praise him with strings and pipe!
> Praise him with sounding cymbals;
>   praise him with loud clashing cymbals!
> Let everything that has breath praise the LORD!
> Praise the LORD!

These instruments were forged from the natural resources from within and surrounding Israel. It is thus the worship of the Israelites

---

29. See, for example, Kariamu Welsh Asante, *African Dance: An Artistic, Historical, and Philosophical Inquiry* (Trenton, NJ: Africa World Press, 1998).

30. Mostafa Vaziri, *Rumi and Shams' Silent Rebellion: Parallels with Vedanta, Buddhism, and Shaivism* (New York: Palgrave Macmillan, 2015), 110.

31. Bakan, *World Music*, 20.

that gives voice to creation's praise of God. In many respects, we can think of instruments as the living transformation of the natural resources of the world, breathing the breath of life into them so as to fulfill the final verse: "Let everything that has breath praise the LORD!"

Similarly, the violins of Antonio Stradivari and the Guarneri family are what the spruce trees of Fiemme Valley in northern Italy would sound like if those trees could sing. The 'Are'are people of Malaita (part of the Solomon Islands) utilize bamboo not only in making their primary melodic instrument, the panpipe, but also as the basic classification category for all their instruments.[32] The Bushmen or San people of the Kalahari Desert make instruments out of their hunting bows with a calabash gourd used as a resonator.[33] Western classical guitars are transformations of cedar, pine, and rosewood. Conversely, modern societies utilize what are called *electronophones*, which generate sound and amplification through electronics.[34] Thus music is a reflection of our ecology, the sounds of the natural or (in the case of modern societies) artificial world around us.

Furthermore, cultures can hear the sounds of creation as indicative of divine song. In Papua New Guinea, Kaluli song makers search for new songs by listening to the sounds of water.[35] The aboriginal Walbiri people believe that once the world was created, the flows of nature had to be stimulated by human rituals of music, art, and dance. Hence, music for the Aborigines functions to restore order and balance in the world and to maintain harmony with nature.[36] In Hinduism, Brahmin priests are obligated to chant what is called the "Gāyatrī Mantra" three times a day, which serves to sonically emphasize the unity between earth, sky, and heaven.[37]

---

32. Bakan, *World Music*, 63.
33. Bakan, *World Music*, 80.
34. Bakan, *World Music*, 71.
35. John Luther Adams, "In Search of an Ecology of Music," http://capress.link/eoe0302.
36. Rappaport, *Ritual*, 460–461.
37. Beck, *Sacred Sound*, 118.

   Chapter Three. What Is Music? Exploring the World of Song

h. Music is spatial.

Music cultivates and shapes distinctive spaces or soundscapes. In chapter 2, we discovered that one of the characteristic features of sonic experiences is that sound involves a kind of independence from its material source. The very fact that we inquire "Where is that sound coming from?" evidences this distinction. Objects do not have sounds in the sense that they have what are called secondary qualities, such as colors. I can perceive a sound without perceiving its source, but I cannot see the color red without seeing a red object of some sort.

Furthermore, as Jeremy Begbie notes, as I look around at the world, everything that I encounter visually is specific to the direction in which I am looking. Whatever I am looking at "here" cannot be seen when I look "there." Visual experience and discreet location become inseparable. "But in aural experience," Begbie writes,

> although a sound may have a discreet material source whose discrete location I can identify . . . the sound I hear is not dependent on attention to that "place." It surrounds me, it fills the whole of my aural "space." I do not hear a sound "there" but "not here"—what I hear occupies the whole of my aural space.[38]

Culturally speaking, few sounds are as constructive of space as the *Adhan*, or Islamic call to prayer. Echoing from atop the minaret, the chanting of the *Adhan* is probably the most powerful sonic symbol of Islamic presence. The aural manifestation of the *Koran*, or "recitation," approximates the language of angels as heard from the mouth of Jibrāʾīl (Gabriel) to the ears of Mohammed.[39] Similarly, the singing of Gregorian chant in the resonance-filled gothic cathedral creates a sonic space wherein the mass of stone appears to be singing. Restaurants are often sonically decorated with a music characteristic

---

38. Begbie, *Theology, Music and Time*, 24. Thus, Begbie concludes that there is the appearance of the attribute of "omnipresence" in music.
39. Qureshi, "Islam and Music," 89.

of the food type: the sounds of sitar in an Indian restaurant, an operatic violin in an Italian restaurant, or classic rock in a bar & grill. Disney's World Showcase at Epcot's tour of the world features (rather cliché) Mexican, German, and Moroccan music to create soundscapes considered representative of these regions.[40]

5. Music and the Numinous

In our last chapter, we heard from the scholar Rudolf Otto on the role of sound in the experience of the numinous or a sense of divine reality. Otto observes the following about music:

> Music, in short, arouses in us an experience and vibrations of mood that are quite specific in kind . . . . The resultant complex mood is, as it were, a fabric, in which the general human feelings and emotional states constitute the warp, and the non-rational music-feelings the woof. . . . The real content of music is not drawn from the ordinary human emotions at all, and . . . is in no way merely a second language, alongside the usual one, by which these emotions find expression. Musical feeling is rather (like numinous feeling) something "wholly other."[41]

Akin to Fubini's observations above, we encounter something in music that is totally unlike any other experience in our lives, what Otto calls something "wholly other."

This goes far in explaining why in all societies, music is found in religious ritual—it is almost everywhere a mainstay of sacred ceremonies— leading some scholars, according to the ethnomusicologist Bruno Nettl, "to suggest that perhaps music was actually invented for humans to have

---

40. On a development of Disney's use of music to create a Disney-like experience, see the illuminative study by Charles Carson, "'Whole New Worlds': Music and the Disney Theme Park Experience," *Ethnomusicology Forum* 13, no. 2 (Nov. 2004): 228–235.
41. Otto, *Idea of the Holy*, 49.

       Chapter Three. What Is Music? Exploring the World of Song

a special way of communicating with the supernatural."[42] It shouldn't surprise us, therefore, that music is the only art or craft in the West that is actually named after a divinity, the *Muses*.

> *In cultures throughout the world,*
> *music uniquely creates an acoustic*
> *atmosphere that can represent sonically the*
> *multidimensional world around us,*
> *which in turn influences and inspires our*
> *souls and bodies, all the while organizing and*
> *structuring our communities and ecologies.*

6. SUMMARY

The eight features of music explored above account at least in part for both the *revelatory* nature of music and its *formative* power to shape and cultivate our humanity. In cultures throughout the world, music uniquely creates an acoustic atmosphere that can represent sonically the multidimensional world around us, which in turn influences and inspires our souls and bodies, all the while organizing and structuring our communities and ecologies.

And yet, we who live and breathe and have our being in the modern Western world, one so devoted to scientific reasoning and technological progress, are highly prone to overlook or ignore this mystical meaning of music. Music for moderns has thus largely lost its formative power, having been relegated to little more than mere subjective sentiment and personal preference.

But it wasn't always this way. Our Western culture once had a profound theology of music rooted in a divine conception of

---

42. Cited in Beck, *Sacred Sound*, 7.

creation which served to nourish and cultivate wisdom and virtue in the human person. In the chapter that follows, I want to explore this theological interplay between music, creation, and humanity, in the hopes that the rediscovery of classical education in our modern age will serve as a conduit for the rediscovery of music and, along with it, a rediscovery of our world and what it means to be truly human.

Questions for Reflection and Discussion

1. Is your definition of music different from Jeremy Begbie's definition? What would you add that he omits?

2. Do you agree with the idea of music's iconicity? Does music have to resemble what it is trying to communicate, or can music be expressive in other ways?

3. How has music marked different periods of time in your own life? For example, think of how music was a central part of various rites of passage or special events.

4. What are some of the most memorable emotional responses you've had toward music? What was it about the piece that elicited such a reaction?

5. Reread the Arthur Schopenhauer quote on page 36 (under "e. Music is emotional."). In what ways does music express emotion itself?

6. In what ways can music bring a community together?

7. What are some examples in which music creates a special sense of space? And how would such a creation affect our experience of the world?

8. Have you ever experienced music in a way that could be described as mystical or mysterious? What made it so?

Chapter Three. What Is Music? Exploring the World of Song

SUGGESTED LISTENING EXERCISE

Listen to musical selections from around the world, specifically for how they exemplify the various features of music. Can you hear a culture's ecology represented by its natural resources turned into instruments? How about its sense of community? What kind of emotions does the music seek to convey? Is it linked with a cultural notion of time?

SUGGESTIONS FOR FURTHER READING

Michael B. Bakan, *World Music: Traditions and Transformations* (New York: McGraw-Hill, 2007).

Guy L. Beck, ed., *Sacred Sound: Experiencing Music in World Religions* (Waterloo, Ontario: Wilfrid Laurier University Press, 2006).

Jeremy S. Begbie, *Theology, Music and Time* (Cambridge: Cambridge University Press, 2000).

Jason Martineau, *The Elements of Music: Melody, Rhythm, and Harmony* (New York: Bloomsbury, 2008).

Roger Scruton, *The Aesthetics of Music* (Oxford: Clarendon Press, 1997).

Kay Kaufman Shelemay, *Soundscapes: Exploring Music in a Changing World* (New York: Norton, 2015).

Christopher Small, *Musicking: The Meanings of Performing and Listening* (Middletown, CT: Wesleyan University Press, 1998).

CHAPTER FOUR
The Melody of Creation:
Music as Cosmic Song

1. INTRODUCTION

We have thus far explored the mysterious world of sound and song. By discovering the various ways in which acoustic environments shape our experience of the world, along with the eight features by which music transfigures such soundscapes, we are better able to appreciate how music reveals an unseen dimension of reality in such a way that shapes profoundly our humanity. But there's a massive stumbling block to the realization and appreciation of this revelatory significance of music in our modern Western world, one that incessantly sequesters music from its sanctifying influence over our lives. In this chapter, I want to explore how I have personally witnessed this obstacle, and provide a summative overview on what was once a profoundly formative conception of music in the Western world, and how such a conception can awaken to shape our lives once again.

2. MUSICAL RELATIVISM

The last notes of the *Sanctus* from the early seventeenth-century English composer William Byrd's *Mass for Four Voices* faded into silence. After turning the CD player off, I sat down in front of about twenty college students. For many, this was their first attentive hearing of Renaissance polyphony.

"So, what do you think?" I asked them.

A hand is raised at the back of the classroom.

"I found it kinda boring."

"OK, but should you have?" I responded.

"What do you mean?" my student asked incredulously. "It's just my opinion."

"I understand, but is your opinion correct?"

Her brows furrowed. "It's music. There is no correct answer. It's all a matter of opinion."

* * *

The musical perspective that dominates our age is what we might call the *relativist* view. The relativist view sees music as entirely personal; there is no objective basis for determining whether one kind or form of music is "better" than another. Music is simply a matter of subjective taste and personal preference, and bears no resemblance at all to the categories that lend themselves to objective evaluation, such as mathematics and the sciences.

This view is profoundly flawed. It is inextricably linked to a consumerist mentality that reduces music to a mere commodity, which is appropriated as a prepackaged formulaic that serves mass utility goals through global distribution channels. The life expectancy of a song in this cultural context is brief, the average radio lifespan being no more than a few months. Indeed, a study was released recently that suggested playing a chart hit for more than four months may adversely affect the ratings of a radio station.[1] This sonic commodification stands in stark contrast to the music of many other cultures outside the West, some of which celebrate tunes and melodies that have lasted for over a thousand years.

---

1. Radioanalyzer, "Overplaying songs is dangerous business," Radioanalyzer.com, http://capress.link/eoe0401.

 Chapter Four. The Melody of Creation: Music as Cosmic Song

Unfortunately, this relativism has not passed over the church, despite its rich musical tradition. A particularly striking example comes from Rick Warren. In his 1995 megahit, *The Purpose Driven Church*, he writes:

> I reject the idea that music styles can be judged as either "good" or "bad" music. Who decides this? The kind of music you like is determined by your background and culture. . . . Churches also need to admit that no particular *style* of music is "sacred." What makes a song sacred is its *message*. Music is nothing more than an arrangement of notes and rhythms; it's the words that make a song spiritual.[2]

According to a 2005 Barna survey of American pastors, *The Purpose Driven Church* was cited as the second most influential book in their lives.[3]

Truth, Goodness, and Beauty are not sequestered from one another—they need one another and they are implied in one another. And if Beauty is robbed of its transcendent nature and relocated solely to cultural and private psychological processes, then Truth and Goodness are sure to follow.

One needs to look no further than our institutions of Christian education to see how pervasive this relativistic view of music has become. I have found that students at both the Christian school and university at which I teach, when called to give a basic account for the classical conception of art and beauty, give answers to my

---

2. Rick Warren, *The Purpose Driven Church: Growth without Compromising Your Message and Mission* (Grand Rapids: Zondervan, 1995), 281.

3. Barna, "Survey Reveals The Books and Authors That Have Most Influenced Pastors," Barna. com, http://capress.link/eoe0402.

inquiries which consistently exemplify a complete and total devotion to aesthetic relativism. I am not exaggerating in the least.

This suggests to me that while we have put much thought into teaching Truth and Goodness particularly in our classical schools, we have done so at the expense of teaching Beauty, and I am very concerned that our educational efforts are in fact being undermined by a ubiquitous relativism coming through the back door. Truth, Goodness, and Beauty are not sequestered from one another—they need one another and they are implied in one another. And if Beauty is robbed of its transcendent nature and relocated solely to cultural and private psychological processes, then Truth and Goodness are sure to follow.[4]

3. FROM CREATION TO NATURE

The relativist view of music is rooted in the assumptions about the world that were forged in the fires of the Enlightenment. It was within this eighteenth-century movement that the world transformed from divine *creation* to impersonal *nature*. Mediated no longer by the pastor and priest but now by the scientist, the world changed from an arena of divine agency and meaning to one governed by chemical, biological, and physical causal laws.

It is here, with this shift from divine creation to impersonal nature, that we begin to see the categories of art and beauty relocated from the objective world to the subjective mind. What we find in the writings of Francis Hutcheson, David Hume, Immanuel Kant, and others, with all their variations, basically boils down to this: we know the world through ideas, and ideas come into the mind through sense perception, which is itself a product of the mind. And one of these

---

4. For a full development of the classical values of Truth, Goodness, and Beauty, see my book *Awakening Wonder: A Classical Guide to Truth, Goodness & Beauty* (Camp Hill, PA: Classical Academic Press, 2015).

ideas that the mind produces is the idea of Beauty. Thus, aesthetic taste is part of an overall internal subjective interpretation of an external world that can only be known by the ideas generated through sense perception. Music and art are thereby transformed into a completely subjective, that is, person-relative category of interpretation.

4. THE MUSIC OF CREATION

The biblical vision of music stands in stark contrast to this relativistic view. Scripture begins with God as creator and the cosmos as creation. The Septuagint, the ancient Greek translation of the Hebrew Scriptures, explicitly links this creative process with Beauty. In the original Hebraic version of the Genesis creation account, a responsive refrain accompanies each one of God's creative actions: "And it was good." The word there for "good" is the Hebrew *tov*. However, when it was translated into the Greek in the third century before Christ, the translators rendered the term for "good" as *kallos*, which not only means "beautiful," but is related etymologically to *kalein*, "to call."

It is this interpretation of Genesis that overlapped with other passages of Scripture to inspire both Jewish and Christian traditions to see God as creating the world as a grand symphony. The book of Job describes how the morning stars sang together and the sons of God shouted for joy as the world was created (38:7). In the Septuagint version of Proverbs, Wisdom was with God holding all things together in harmony (8:30).[5] This vision of the world created through heavenly song captured the imagination of C.S. Lewis when he wrote *The Magician's Nephew*, where Aslan sings Narnia into being, creating the world through song.

Throughout the Old Testament, the creation itself is depicted as a great Temple in which worship is to be done—God sets the foun-

5. Margaret Barker, "Temple Music," http://capress.link/eoe0403.

dations, he stretches the heavens as a canopy, and we are here to pick up on that song of creation and make it manifest, make it audible in the world (cf. Psalm 104). The "new song" (cf. Psalms 93, 96, 98) that resounded in the House of the Lord echoed the heavenly song that awakened the world into being, and thus perpetuated the life of creation.

> *Pythagoras envisioned the harmoniousness of the whole universe, such that each of these planets and star systems has its own different tonal sequence. And thus it is the combination of the stars and the planets that make the sounds of the heavenly spheres.*

Music for the Jewish imagination thus revealed the world to be an arena of divine creation. Indeed, it could be viewed that music was itself a manifestation of the presence of God. Upon the return of the Ark of the Covenant to the tabernacle, the Chronicler describes how David appointed musicians "to invoke, to thank, and to praise the Lord, the God of Israel" (1 Chron. 16:4). Once Solomon's temple was finished, the Levitical choir praised and thanked the Lord "with one voice," and then the glory of the Lord filled the temple (2 Chron. 5:11-14). As we noted above, the connection between music and the presence of God may be found in the Hebrew term for "praise," *hll*, which also means "shine." The music of the Levitical choir thus invoked the radiance of the presence of God.

5. THE MUSIC OF THE SPHERES

The Hebrews were not alone in conceiving of the cosmos as an arena of divine song. The Ionian Greek philosopher Pythagoras (ca. 570–490 BC) imagined that the entire cosmos is subject to the same laws of proportion that rule music, such that all things form a great harmony. This term, *harmonia*, for the Greeks is not so much a musical term as it is a cosmic one. Harmony is first and foremost a cosmic mathematical principle which involves a blending and combining of opposites into a grand system, a cosmic structure where all things are related to each other. Pythagoras linked together the mathematics that comprise the basis for music with the idea that there are underlying mathematical harmonies throughout the entire cosmos to come up with his concept of the "music of the spheres." Pythagoras envisioned the harmoniousness of the whole universe, such that each of these planets and star systems has its own different tonal sequence. And thus it is the combination of the stars and the planets that make the sounds of the heavenly spheres.

The important point here is that music for the Greeks and the wider classical tradition was not so much understood as something performed, composed, practiced, or played; rather, music was interpreted as a mathematical discipline that sought to discover and formalize the symmetrical relations between sounds.[6] It was an integral component to the mathematical disciplines that comprised the *quadrivium*: arithmetic, geometry, music, and astronomy. For the classical mind, arithmetic revealed "number in itself," geometry revealed "number in space," music revealed "number in time," and astronomy revealed "number in space and time." In this sense, music was an integral part of the Greek educational curriculum which functioned as a metaphor for this whole cosmic chain of interrelationships and harmonies. Indeed, Plato could say: "The whole choral art is also in our view the whole of education" (*Laws*, Bk II). The Greeks understood the nature of reality and its systems of relations in musical terms.

---

6. Carol Harrison, "Augustine and the Art of Music," in *Resonant Witness: Conversations between Music and Theology*, ed. Jeremy S. Begbie and Steve R. Guthrie (Grand Rapids: Eerdmans, 2011), 27.

6. THE CHRISTIAN REAPPROPRIATION

Christian apologists such as Clement of Alexandria (ca. 150–ca. 215 AD) reshaped the Pythagorean concept of the music of the spheres by presenting Christ as "the minstrel who imparts harmony to the universe and makes music to God."[7] Inspired by cosmic passages such as John 1:1, 1 Corinthians 8:6, and Colossians 1:15-20, they posited that the symphony of the cosmos is in fact Christ, the *Logos*, through whom all things were made and in whom all things hold together. Clement's successor, Origen, envisioned a cosmic chorus in Christian worship:

> For we sing hymns to the one God who is over all and
> his only begotten Word, who is God also. So we sing
> to God and his only begotten as do the sun, the moon,
> the stars and the entire heavenly host. For all these
> form a sacred chorus and sing hymns to the God of
> all and his only begotten along with those among men
> who are just. (*Against Celsus* VIII, 67)[8]

Augustine (354–430) developed this even further in his *De Musica* with the conception that the numbers of music derive from the unchanging order of eternal numbers which themselves proceed from God. Indeed, Augustine concludes his study in Book VI with the insight that God *is* music. In other words, God *is* perfect symmetry, proportionality, unity, diversity, harmony, and number.[9] For Augustine, when God formed the world from nothing, the *form* was itself music. Thus the entire chain of created being is held together and sustained by music. And we are obligated to maintain and perpetuate that harmony as creatures wholly dependent on the promises and provisions of our Creator.

---

7. Avery Cardinal Dulles, *A History of Apologetics* (Eugene, OR: Wipf and Stock Publishers, 1997), 39–40.
8. Cited in James McKinnon, *Music in Early Christian Literature* (Cambridge: Cambridge University Press, 1987), 38.
9. Harrison, "Augustine," 31.

     Chapter Four. The Melody of Creation: Music as Cosmic Song

And it all came together with the music theory of Boethius (480–524) in the early sixth century. In his *Principles of Music*, he structured music according to the threefold pattern of the music of the spheres, the music of the natural world, and the music of the soul. His treatise, which was transmitted throughout the Latin West, was inordinately influential for the next thousand years. Indeed, Boethius's *Principles of Music* was the music theory textbook used at Oxford until as recently as 1856.[10]

In Jewish, Greek, and Christian traditions, the goal of music was to reveal reality by awakening on earth the music of the heavens, that is, the numbers, symmetries, consonances, and unities of the cosmos. While we can't hear this cosmic music (in that we are too far and fallen), we do have access to the mathematics and principles of symmetry by which that music constantly sounds. This is reflected in the Greek word *symmetria*, which means "beautiful." By awakening the music of the heavens on earth through the study of mathematical proportionality and symmetry, we are able to embody such cosmic harmony and thus transform into heavenly beings.

7. Music and the Sanctification of the Soul

This *transformative* significance of music is key. Music was considered a divinely ordained instrument for the sanctification of the soul.[11] Plato's pursuit of the Good in his *Republic* outlines his *musikē paideia*, how music and poetry provide the chief means by which rhythm and harmony could be communicated through the body and sunk deeply

---

10. Robert Reilly, "The Music of the Spheres," http://capress.link/eoe0404.
11. This is often referred to as the "doctrine of ethos" in Hellenistic musical thought and practice. See Donald Jay Grout, J. Peter Burkholder, and Claude V. Palisca, *A History of Western Music* (New York: Norton, 2001), 6.

into the recesses of the soul.[12] And because the Beauty of music communicates Truth and Goodness to the whole soul, bringing harmony to our rational, volitional, and aesthetic capacities, the music of the cosmos always involves the awakening of *arête*, the classical virtues (wisdom, moderation, justice, and courage), which results when the intellectual, moral, and emotional constituents of our souls reflect the balance or harmony of the cosmos (cf. *Republic* 442A).[13]

Within this cosmic and intellectual milieu, the early church developed a profound sense of the *formative* significance of music for the human person. Athanasius's extended discussion of the psalms observes that singing was ordained to benefit the soul, "because as harmony creates a single concord in joining together the two pipes of the aulos, so . . . reason will that a man be not disharmonious with himself, nor at variance with himself" (*Epistula ad Marcellinum de interpretatione psalmorum* 27).[14] The facilitation of this inner harmony is a necessary constituent of music: "Just as we make known and signify the thoughts of the soul through the words we express, so too the Lord wished the melody of the words to be a sign of the spiritual harmony of the soul, and ordained that the canticles be sung with melody and the psalms read with song" (*Epistula ad Marcellinum* 28).[15]

Basil of Caesarea understood the psalms as a chief means of shaping a wise and harmonious soul: "Thus he [the Holy Spirit] contrived for us these harmonious psalm tunes, so that those who are children in actual age as well as those who are young in behavior, while appearing only to sing would in reality be training their souls" (*Homilia in psalmum i*).[16] In the same sermon, Basil spoke of a psalm as "tranquility of soul and the arbitration of peace; it settles one's

---

12. Andrew Louth, *The Origins of the Christian Mystical Tradition: From Plato to Denys* (Oxford: Oxford University Press, 1981), 8.

13. For a helpful overview of the classical conception of *harmonia* and its relationship to virtue, see Basil Cole, *Music and Morals: A Theological Appraisal of the Moral and Psychological Effects of Music* (Staten Island, NY: Alba House, 1993), 15–45.

14. Cited in McKinnon, *Music*, 53.

15. Cited in McKinnon, *Music*, 53.

16. Cited in McKinnon, *Music*, 65.

 Chapter Four. The Melody of Creation: Music as Cosmic Song

tumultuous and seething thoughts. It mollifies the soul's wrath and chastens its recalcitrance."[17] And in his letter to youth, Basil contrasted the ethos engendered by different types of music:

> The passions born of illiberality and baseness of spirit are naturally occasioned by this sort of music. But we must pursue that other kind, which is better and leads to the better, and which, as they say, was used by David, that author of sacred songs, to soothe the king in his madness. And it is said that Pythagoras, upon encountering some drunken revelers, commanded the aulete [a player of an aulos, an ancient Greek wind instrument] who was leading their song to change the mode and to play the Dorian for them. They were so sobered by this music that tearing off their garlands they returned home ashamed. . . . Such is the difference in filling one's ears with wholesome or wicked tunes![18]

Along with Augustine's insight above on the obligatory nature of music, we can see that music was considered profoundly *moral* for the formative period of the church. Music was either oriented away from God and toward demons, or it was oriented back toward God within a redeemed cosmic order through the redemptive work of Christ. The job of the composer is to reveal the world as recreated in Christ and thereby facilitate the sanctification of the soul in the cultivation of wisdom and virtue. To the extent that our musical tastes and sensibilities are in the service of this larger cosmic reality, they are reflective of this redemptive vision.

* * *

> Teach me the songs of thy truth,
>   that I may yield fruits in thee;
> And open the cithara of thy Holy Spirit to me,
>   that with every note I may praise thee, O Lord.
>
>   (*Odes of Solomon* XIV, 7–8)[19]

---

17. Cited in McKinnon, *Music*, 65.
18. Cited in Cole, *Music and Morals*, 55.
19. Cited in McKinnon, *Music*, 23.

8. Music: Then and Now

I lament that this vision of sonic revelation has all but disappeared in the life of the church. The Jewish, Greek, and Christian worlds had a *fundamentally* different understanding of music than we modern Christians do. When they spoke of music, they thought of it in a very different way than we do. Music historically understood was no more a matter of mere taste and preference than were the physical laws of the universe. Nor was it composed, practiced, and distributed as a commodity for the consumptive habits of market-driven demographics. Neither was music reduced to mere melody and rhythm with its meaning limited solely to words. Music, particularly in the Christian tradition, revealed the interrelated intricacies of the world as divine creation, and was a facilitator of sanctification and redemption, which operated much like a divine physics that awakened and attracted the soul to beatific life. Music revealed the fact that the cosmos was indeed a grand design, a moral world dependent upon a divine creator for its origin and sustenance.

In many respects, then, recovering the classical Christian vision of music involves nothing less than rediscovering the lost *world* to which such music is wedded. The world of the Jewish and Christian imaginations involved a divine theater of creation and revelation. The world of the modern imagination involves a vast network of physical, chemical, and biological processes that have no meaning or purpose apart from that which we choose to impose upon them. Classical Christians believed in creation, we moderns believe in nature; their life centered on the sacraments, ours centers on secular science.

The irony, of course, is that the purposeless world indicative of our modern age is not the world that gave us Bach and therefore is not responsible for the Beatles either; in the case of both, there were some objective principles of music making forged in the sonic life of the church from which they could draw. By relativizing music, by perpetuating the idea that all musical standards are mere personal preference, we undermine the very frames of reference that gave us the music we currently enjoy in the first place.

I like reminding my students that virtually all of the music that they hear on the radio is Christian. Of course I am initially greeted with skepticism. But that is only because they assume the *meaning* of music as represented by modern sensibilities: meaning resides in the lyrics. A song is Christian only insofar as it has Christian *words* or is the product of a Christian composer. But the music that constitutes our Top 40 song lists exemplifies tonal and harmonic structures that have a history, and at the center of that history is the church and its development of Jewish and Greek musical traditions. From one end of the radio dial spectrum to the other, that tonal tradition continues.

9. Summary

In his prequel to his grand epic, *The Lord of the Rings*, J.R.R. Tolkien described the creation of Middle-earth in *The Silmarillion* by the god Eru Ilúvatar. Eru gives to the angels a melody that they are able to develop and express in a cosmic song: "I will now that ye make in harmony together a Great Music. . . . I will sit and hearken, and be glad that through you great beauty has been awakened into song."[20] As those who inhabit the modern age, we are rather deaf to this call to awaken beauty into song. We've been highly conditioned to reinterpret music as little more than a mere commodity dictated by personal preference and subjective taste. And yet we are, often unknowingly, the heirs of a profound theology of music rooted in a divine conception of creation, one that cultivated and continues to nourish wisdom and virtue for all those who hearken unto its call.

While the Greek and particularly Pythagorean musical tradition provided the early church with a music theory connecting the

---

20. J.R.R. Tolkien, *The Silmarillion* (London: Allen and Unwin, 1977), 15.

harmony of the cosmos with the ethical formation of the soul, that musical tradition fell short of providing the *conceptual content* for such a theory. Christians drew deeply from the Hebrew Scriptures in order to shape what would be a distinctively Christian musical theology, and it is to that musical theology we now turn.

QUESTIONS FOR REFLECTION AND DISCUSSION

1. Do you see musical relativism as a problem today? How have you encountered aesthetic relativism, or perhaps how are you practicing it?

2. How do we experience musical relativism in the church today?

3. Is musical elitism the only alternative to musical relativism? If not, how do we avoid such elitism?

4. Do you think it's possible for us to think of Beauty as solely a matter of personal opinion without it affecting adversely our conceptions of Truth and Goodness?

5. How did the Enlightenment change our conception of the world?

6. What similarities do you observe between the ancient Hebrew conception of music and the Greek conception?

7. The Greeks appropriated music as a form of mathematics. What similarities do music and mathematics share?

8. How did the ancient Christian conception of music bring together the Jewish and Greek conceptions?

9. Do you believe that music is capable of influencing our moral decisions? If so, how?

 Chapter Four. The Melody of Creation: Music as Cosmic Song

Suggested Listening Exercise

Listen to the *Sanctus* from William Byrd's *Mass for Four Voices* and discuss the piece in relation to the musical theology learned in this chapter. Notice, for example, the melodic direction of the voices ascending upward in prayer, as well as the unity in diversity among the various voices reflecting the unity in diversity in the fellowship of the Trinity.

Suggestions for Further Reading

Augustine, "*De Musica,*" *The Fathers of the Church, Vol. 4*, trans. Robert Taliaferro (Washington, DC: Catholic University of America Press, 1947).

Basil Cole, *Music and Morals: A Theological Appraisal of the Moral and Psychological Effects of Music* (Staten Island, NY: Alba House, 1993).

Boethius, *The Consolation of Philosophy*, trans. Richard H. Green (Mineola, NY: Dover Publications, 2002).

Boethius, *The Fundamentals of Music*, trans. Calvin M. Bower (New Haven, CT: Yale University Press, 1989).

Joscelyn Godwin, *Harmonies of Heaven and Earth: The Spiritual Dimensions of Music from Antiquity to the Avant-Garde* (Rochester, VT: Inner Traditions International, 1987).

Joscelyn Godwin, ed., *The Harmony of the Spheres: A Sourcebook of the Pythagorean Tradition in Music* (Rochester, VT: Inner Traditions International, 1993).

Robert Reilly, "The Music of the Spheres," http://capress.link/eoe0404.

Férdia J. Stone-Davis, *Musical Beauty: Negotiating the Boundary between Subject and Object* (Eugene, OR: Cascade Books, 2011).

Chapter Five
The Song of the Seraphim:
Music as Echoes of Paradise

1. Introduction

In the preceding chapters, I have argued that music is revelatory in nature. The sonic world discloses to us a world unseen, making perceptible the imperceptible, or visible the invisible, as it were. Through rhythmic depictions of time, the sonority of space, the harmonies of fellowship and community, the instrumental transformation of ecology, and the transfiguration of the dancing body, music awakens us to a reality otherwise hidden, which profoundly shapes ourselves and our lifeworlds. For the Greeks, Jews, and Christians, this revelatory significance of music involved manifesting on earth the music of the heavens, that is, the numbers, symmetries, consonances, and unities of the cosmos. Such awakening in turn served to cultivate wisdom and virtue within the listener, who thereby participated in the harmony of the cosmos, thus becoming truly human.

We have yet to explore the distinctively Christian contribution to this cosmic vision of music. In what follows, we'll discover the unique musical vision of early Christians that reimagined the sonic worlds of the Jews and Greeks in terms of the transformative life, death, and resurrection of Jesus Christ.

2. The Sounds of Paradise

For over a decade now, my family and I have been part of the Eastern Orthodox communion. The particular church to which we belong, the Greek Orthodox Church, maintains one of the earliest Christian musical traditions, sacred chant. When one enters into such a soundscape, one is eventually struck by the unique duality of the chant. One cantor sings the melody while the other drones a single tone, called the *isokratema*. The purpose of the melody is to interpret the words of the hymn text, what the Greeks would call a melodic *kerygma*, the word for "preaching" or "proclaiming." The purpose of the single-note drone is to represent the in-breaking of eternity into time, the infinite source of the *kerygma*.

The sonic interweaving of time and eternity in Byzantine song is indicative of a profoundly enchanting narrative of aural redemption, where heaven and earth come together into a musical harmony that is revealed through the transformative life, death, and resurrection of Christ.

Piecing together early Christian music theory is quite the challenge; the evidence remains rather thin and sporadic, particularly in the New Testament (cf. Eph. 5:19; Col. 3:16; Rev. 14:2-3). What is often overlooked is that in addition to the canonical texts of sacred scripture, there are a number of early Jewish and Christian writings that contemporary scholars call *pseudepigraphal* and *apocalyptic* texts. Not many of us are familiar with these works, but they are profound windows into the kind of moral imagination taking shape among some of the Christians during the early period of the church. One of these texts is entitled *The Testament of Adam*, which scholars date to the middle or late third century AD.[1] The *Testament* purports to be a transcript of the final words of Adam, which culminate in his prophecy of the coming of Christ. Of interest is how it begins by

---

1. "Testamentum Adami," Internet Sacred Text Archive, http://capress.link/eoe0501.

 Chapter Five. The Song of the Seraphim: Music as Echoes of Paradise

describing the sonic atmosphere to which Adam was privy in the garden before he sinned. According to the *Testament*, Adam was able to hear the praises of the seraphim and the angels in the garden, who sang at certain times in the day, which constituted a sonic manifestation of the unity of heaven and earth. But having been expelled from the garden, the heavenly music was silenced in our world, evidencing our cosmic estrangement from Paradise.

This sacred sound is approximated, albeit in polluted form, in the various musics of the world. A common refrain in early Christian literature is that music, particularly instrumental music, has been perverted. The harmony of the cosmos has been interrupted, and thus the universe is experiencing dissonance and discord as found in the music of Jubal, the descendant of Cain, and developed by the Egyptians and Greeks. Cyril of Jerusalem (ca. 315–386) gave a particularly poignant example, where he saw the serpent reappearing into the world through music and musical instruments and gestures:

> In fact the aulos itself is an imitation of the serpent through which the Evil One spoke and tricked Eve. For it was in imitation of that type that the aulos was made, for the purpose of deceiving mankind. And observe the type, which he who plays the aulos represents upon the instrument. For the player throws his head back, then bows forward; he inclines to the right, then similarly to the left. (*Panarion* XXV, 4)[2]

The ancient Jewish perspective appears to concur. With the noise pollution of a fallen world, the soundscape of heaven could only be heard through divinely granted visions of heaven or *apocalyptics*. Centuries before *The Testament of Adam*, Isaiah recorded a similar vision, where God's throne was surrounded by seraphim calling out the *Trisagion*, "Holy, holy, holy is the LORD of hosts; the whole earth is full of his glory!" (Isa. 6:3). Comparably, in the inaugural vision of

---

2. Cited in McKinnon, *Music*, 78.

Ezekiel, he heard the wings of the living beings surrounding God's throne, which sounded "like the voice of the Almighty" (Ezek. 1:24, NASB). Again later he equated "the sound of the wings of the cherubim" with "the voice of God Almighty when He speaks" (10:5).

Evidently inspired by Isaiah and Ezekiel, a subsequent Jewish tradition emerged which imagined Abraham encountering this heavenly music. *The Apocalypse of Abraham*, an extracanonical text written approximately in the second century AD and preserved by Christians, tells the story of Abraham being caught up into heaven during his sacrificial worship and guided by an angel who is identified as the "Singer of the Eternal One" (12:4).[3] The angel proceeds to teach Abraham to sing the song of the angels:

> And the angel said, "Worship, Abraham, and utter the song which I shall now teach you. Utter it without ceasing, that is, without pause, in one continuous strain from beginning to end." And the song which he taught me to sing had words appropriate to that sphere in which we then stood, for each sphere in heaven has its own song of praise, and only those who dwell there know how to utter it, and those upon earth cannot know or utter it except they be taught by the messengers of heaven. (*Apocalypse of Abraham* 17:19)

In teaching Abraham how to sing the song, the angel revealed the harmony of the cosmic order (*Apocalypse of Abraham* 18:11; 19:9).[4]

This connection between song and the presence of God in the apocalyptic imagination seems to have been nurtured in the music of the Levitical choirs of King David.[5] Upon the return of the Ark of the Covenant, the Levitical choirs burst into song, heralding the return of God's presence among his people (1 Chron. 16:4). In 2 Chronicles 5, the completion of Solomon's temple is accompanied

---

3. *The Apocalypse of Abraham*, Pseudepigrapha.com, http://capress.link/eoe0502.
4. Margaret Barker, *Temple Themes*, 224–225.
5. See the fine study by Peter J. Leithart, *From Silence to Son: The Davidic Liturgical Revolution* (Moscow, ID: Canon Press, 2003).

by Levitical song that does not merely celebrate but actually invokes the presence of God:

> And when the priests came out of the Holy Place (. . . with cymbals, harps, and lyres, [they] stood east of the altar with 120 priests who were trumpeters; and it was the duty of the trumpeters and singers to make themselves heard in unison in praise and thanksgiving to the Lord), and when the song was raised, with trumpets and cymbals and other musical instruments, in praise to the Lord, "For he is good, for his steadfast love endures forever," the house, the house of the Lord, was filled with a cloud, so that the priests could not stand to minister because of the cloud, for the glory of the Lord filled the house of God. (2 Chron. 5:11-14)

And it is with the restoration of temple worship by Hezekiah that we are told that this music of the tabernacle/temple was by divine revelation:

> And he [Hezekiah] stationed the Levites in the house of the Lord with cymbals, harps, and lyres, according to the commandment of David and of Gad the king's seer and of Nathan the prophet; for the commandment was from the Lord through his prophets. (2 Chron. 29:25)

3. THE HERALDS OF HEAVEN: THE SOUNDSCAPE OF THE CHURCH

Against the backdrop of Israel's subsequent exile, we can appreciate the significance of angelic song on the night of the birth of Christ, the Son of David, for it is with the birth of Christ that these sounds of heaven—encountered by visions and approximated by the temple—return explicitly back into the world. From the region of Bethlehem, the song of the seraphim and the angelic choirs that were silenced in our world because of Adam's fall and Israel's exile began to resound throughout the entire world. Hence, the angelic host sang of the reunification of heaven and earth in Christ: "Glory to God in the highest, and on earth peace, good will toward men" (Luke 2:14, KJV). Similarly, in his heavenly vision, John describes how "every creation which is in heaven, and on the earth, and under the earth, and such as are in the sea," praised God, saying: "Blessing, and honour, and glory, and power, be unto him that sitteth upon the throne, and unto the Lamb for ever and ever" (Rev. 5:13, KJV).

For early Christians, this symphonic reunification of heaven and earth *was* the soundscape of the shared lifeworld of the church. Eusebius recorded how Ignatius of Antioch in the second century received a vision of angels singing to God in alternative chant and subsequently introduced antiphonal singing to the church at Antioch (*Church History* 6.8). In his letter to Gregory of Nazianzus (ca. 330–390), Basil of Caesarea (ca. 330–379) described how the monastic practice of sanctifying the hours of prayer each day with singing imitated on earth the chorus of angels in heaven. Gregory himself described the singing in his church as more angelic than human (Oration XLIII, *In laudem Basilii Magni*). He talked of the role of singing in Christian worship as uniting the Christian community on earth with the angels of heaven and thus exemplifying the harmony of creation (*Carmina* 2.1.1.180). Gregory of Nyssa (ca. 335–394), in a Christmas sermon, conceived of creation as "the temple of the Lord of creation" that was sung into being, and it was this divine song that was to be echoed in the hymns of praise among God's people but has been silenced by sin.[6] As a result of the work of Christ, however, people excluded by sin could now rejoin the liturgy of heaven and earth, and in so doing enter into the holy of holies to worship with the angels.

The church in Jerusalem seems to have been particularly drawn to this apocalyptic theology of music. In his *Catechesis*, Cyril of Jeru-

6. Barker, *Temple Themes*, 225.

     Chapter Five. The Song of the Seraphim: Music as Echoes of Paradise

salem wrote how the singers of the church imitate the angelic hosts (XIII, 26). And in his *Mystagogical Catechesis*, he wrote:

> We call to mind the Seraphim also, whom Isaiah saw in the Holy Spirit, present in a circle about the throne of God, covering their faces with two wings, their feet with two, and flying with two, and saying: "Holy, holy, holy is the Lord of hosts" (Isa. 6:3). Therefore we recite this doxology transmitted to us by the Seraphim, in order to become participants in the hymnody of the super terrestrial hosts. (V. 6)[7]

In Antioch, John Chrysostom (ca. 347–407) described the morning practice of singing the "Gloria in excelsis" among monastics as being identical with the choir of angels in heaven (*In Matthaeum*, Hom. LXVIII, 3). And in his *Homilia I in Oziam seu de Seraphinis* 1, he wrote:

> Above, the hosts of angels sing praise; below, men form choirs in the churches and imitate them by singing the same doxology. Above, the Seraphim cry out the Trisagion Hymn ["Holy, holy, holy"]; below, the human throng sends up the same cry. The inhabitants of heaven and earth are brought together in a common solemn assembly; there is one thanksgiving, one shout of delight, one joyful chorus.[8]

In his exposition of Paul's words in Col. 3:16, "Teach and admonish one another with . . . psalms, hymns and spiritual songs," Chrysostom made a distinction between psalms and hymns: "The psalms contain all things, but hymns in turn have nothing human. When one is instructed in the psalms, he will then know hymns also, as a more divine thing. For the powers above sing hymns, they do not sing psalms" (*In Colossenses*, Hom. IX, 2).[9]

---

7. Cited in McKinnon, *Music*, 76.
8. Cited in McKinnon, *Music*, 89.
9. Cited in McKinnon, *Music*, 87.

Having come down from heaven (John 6:38), Christ thus brought with him the *sounds* of heaven, the song of the seraphim, quite literally the music of God, to re-enchant the earth with his heavenly glory and thereby reunite heaven and earth in a symphony of redemption. It was this redemptive narrative that seems to have profoundly shaped the soundscape of the early church. It is the commission of the church to re-enchant the world with the soundscape of heaven, thus witnessing audibly to the reunification of heaven and earth in Christ. Bishop Ambrose of Milan (337–397) played on the connection between the Latin words *canticum* (chant) and *incantator* (enchanter) in his response to the music of the pagan cult when he wrote:

> Many provoke the church, but the charms (*carmina*) of the soothsayer's art are not able to harm her. Those who enchant (*incantatores*) avail not where the chant (*canticum*) of Christ is sung (*decantatur*) daily. The Church has her own enchanter (*incantatorem*), the Lord Jesus, by whom she has voided the spells of the magical charmers and the venom of serpents. (*Hexaemeron* IV, 8.33)[10]

The music of the church "voids" the perverted harmonies of the world with a new harmony, a cosmic symphony between heaven and earth revealed in Christ. It is this Christocentric melody that is to permeate every square inch of the world in order to prepare time and space for its future transfiguration when Christ returns.

This, for me, is why teaching our children to sing is so crucial to cultivating them in the Christian faith. The garden of sound that

---

10. Cited in Carol Harrison, "Psalms Revisited" (unpublished paper), n.p.

   Chapter Five. The Song of the Seraphim: Music as Echoes of Paradise

surrounds us as we sing together the harmonies of a psalm, hymn, or chant awakens us to the restored harmony between heaven and earth returned to us in Christ. Ambrose wrote:

> A psalm joins those with differences, unites those at odds and reconciles those who have been offended, for who will not concede to him with whom one sings to God in one voice? It is after all a great bond of unity for the full number of people to join in one chorus. The strings of the cithara differ, but create one harmony (*symphonia*). The fingers of a musician often go astray among the strings though they are very few in number, but among the people the Spirit musician knows not how to err. (*Explanatio psalmi* I, 9)[11]

I believe Ambrose. I believe that in singing our sacred songs we are indeed participating in the unifying cosmic sounds of the Holy Spirit, which are even now recalibrating time and space around Christ.

* * *

At the end of the meal we traditionally refer to as the Last Supper, we are told that Jesus and the disciples went to the Mount of Olives "when they had sung a hymn" (Matt. 26:30; Mark 14:26). There has been much conjecture as to what precisely that hymn was, many opting for the *Hallel* or Psalms 113–118, which were sung traditionally at the Passover meal. I'm not so interested in the song selection per se. Rather, I can't help but hear that hymn as a sonic gateway into the garden to which Jesus and his disciples subsequently journeyed, a gateway that led the disciples—and through them the whole world—to encounter a cross bridging the cosmic chasm between heaven and earth, and as such, returning us to the Tree of Life.

---

11. Cited in Harrison, "Psalms Revisited," n.p.

4. Summary

Throughout our exploration of music, we have found that the classical imagination hears music as a *mediator*, a revelation of divine meaning and purpose. For the Greeks, the ratios of music disclosed the divinely authored patterns of perfection upon which the whole cosmos was modeled. For the Jews, Levitical song in the temple invoked the very presence of God. Early Christians tapped into both the Greek and Jewish musical traditions, but recalibrated such conception around the redemptive vision of Christ. Having come down from heaven, Christ thus brought with him the *sounds* of heaven, restoring the original soundscape of Paradise wherein the angelic beings daily praised God, thereby witnessing audibly to the reunification of heaven and earth in himself. It was the music of the church that echoed this cosmic reunification, with songs that sought to re-enchant the world with heavenly soundscape. Over the next millennium, this acoustic redemption served to awaken throughout the Western world the greatest and grandest music ever written.

And yet the church today seems largely oblivious to this distinctively Christian musical tradition. In the modern evangelical church, contemporary choruses are more and more substituting for classical hymns, praise bands have replaced choirs, and the guitar is the new organ. All of this raises the question: Has the modern church largely turned its back on its redemptive vision of music? If so, what are the consequences for a distinctively Christian vision of humanity and redemptive life? These are the questions that we shall address in our next chapter.

Questions for Reflection and Discussion

1. Name some ways in which the various musics of the world might be approximations of heavenly music. In what ways

would, for example, pop music be faithful to heavenly music, and in what ways would it be unfaithful?

2. Based on what we learned in both chapters 4 and 5, how would the created order exemplify the kind of music heard in heaven? How might this apply to the moral or ethical effects of music?

3. How do we see the relationship between music and God's presence in the Bible?

4. We read throughout Scripture that God's mighty acts are not to be merely studied, but *praised* (Ps. 145:4; 150:2). Read Eph. 5:19 and Col. 3:16. How would music fulfill this call to praise and delight in God and his works?

5. In what ways do you see the church as faithful to her call to enchant the world with the music of heaven? In what ways is the church falling short of such a call?

Suggested Listening Exercise

Listen to a selection of Byzantine chant, such as the one found here: http://capress.link/eoe0503. Reflect on how Byzantine music is different from, say, contemporary Christian music. For example, can you hear the difference between Byzantine and contemporary spirituality?

Suggestions for Further Reading

Miikka E. Anttila, *Luther's Theology of Music: Spiritual Beauty and Pleasure* (Berlin: Walter de Gruyter, 2013).

Gerald Hobbs, "Christianity and Music," in *Sacred Sound: Experiencing Music in World Religions*, ed. Guy L. Beck (Waterloo, Ontario: Wilfrid Laurier University Press, 2006), 61–88.

James McKinnon, *Music in Early Christian Literature* (Cambridge: Cambridge University Press, 1987).

Johannes Quasten, *Music and Worship in Pagan and Christian Antiquity*, trans. Boniface Ramsey, O.P. (Washington, DC: National Association of Pastoral Musicians, 1983).

John Arthur Smith, *Music in Ancient Judaism and Early Christianity* (Farnham, Surrey: Ashgate, 2011).

Egon Wellesz, *A History of Byzantine Music and Hymnography* (Oxford: Clarendon Press, 1961).

Chapter Six
Rock 'n' Roll Music and the Church:
A Morally Ambiguous Reunion

1. Introduction

Thus far, we've had much to say about a classical conception of music. Historically, music was a sacramental bridge that drew together our world with an eternal one, redeeming our senses and transforming our souls to love what is truly lovely and desire what is truly desirable, thereby enabling us to be truly human. But what about more popular conceptions of music? Given the prominence of contemporary Christian music (CCM) in today's houses of worship, we would be remiss not to address what our assessment might involve when applied to contemporary and popular music.

Given that this is a classical guide to music, I want to examine one particular facet of CCM rather overlooked by many: the *moral ambiguity* inherent in the genre. I must say at the outset that, first, this is most certainly a critical posture but, secondly, I do not believe this criticism is all there is to be said about CCM, and it does not deplete my disposition toward pop music in general. I have played actively in rock bands in the past, and I remain today very much a fan of rock music and heavy metal, and am an ardent admirer of many of its musicians, some of whom are simply stunning virtuosos. That said, our distinctively *moral* assessment of music, as found particularly in chapter 4, requires an ethical evaluation of CCM that needs to be understood and reckoned with if the church is going to faithfully and musically thrive.

2. CCM and Secular Culture

The contemporary evangelical church is, in a word, a rockin' church. Walking into houses of worship today, we often see the sanctuary replaced by a stage, stained glass windows substituted by stage lighting, pews swapped with stadium seating, and the altar exchanged with a drum set.

In many respects, it is secular culture and practices that have informed CCM, and thus many churches. Many CCM artists emulate the broader secular culture, supporting secular sexual ethics such as gay marriage (e.g., Ray Boltz, Jars of Clay, Jennifer Knapp). Even some superstar country Christian artists have expressed support for gay marriage (Dolly Parton, Carrie Underwood); one CCM artist (Trey Pearson of Everyday Sunday) has come out as gay with support from his fans, and even his wife, whom he divorced. Likewise, some CCM artists also support transgender policies that require institutions (such as schools) to acknowledge the declared gender identity of anyone who wishes to be regarded as female, though born male, or as a male, though born female.

Some CCM artists have also adopted common secular performance practices, generally dressing and behaving as secular musicians and imitating their musical tastes and style. One Christian father and former pastor (Patrick Hess) describes bringing his son to a very large Christian music festival (Winter Jam) in 2012 in which some 10,000 concert goers were present and who "screamed uncontrollably" when a youth pastor played clips of secular artists (Justin Bieber and One Direction), leaving Hess to eventually wonder why "the Christian music industry didn't have an alternative to those artists which provided godly lyrics and lived a holy lifestyle."[1] Hess then notes how the recording industry itself is sometimes willing to record some CCM artists that are living quite secular lives indeed.

---

1. Patrick Hess, "Christians in the Music Industry," *Huffpost* (blog), December 30, 2014, https://www.huffingtonpost.com/patrick-hess/christians-in-the-music-i_b_6069488.html.

Such reports are common enough, and known to anyone immersed in the CCM world. The sad fact is that secular culture has set the tone for most of CCM rather than Christians notably impacting the music of the broader culture, much less setting the tone for it.

What's going on here? Why are so many (though not all) contemporary Christian artists either endorsing or manifesting secularized values and lifestyles? In order to answer this, we have to explore the history and aesthetics of rock 'n' roll.[2]

3. THE CHURCH OF ROCK

Many people don't realize that rock music actually came out of the Southern Pentecostal church in the early 1950s. The church served as the space for blending together the three main musical genres that syncretized into rock 'n' roll: African rhythm (placing a primacy on drums), rhythm and blues instrumentation (namely the guitar), and gospel melodies and progressions. The first rock 'n' roll stars all came out of this Southern Pentecostal space: Elvis Presley, Jerry Lee Lewis (the cousin of Jimmy Swaggart), and Little Richard. In fact, Little Richard's song "Tutti Frutti," with its iconic refrain "Awopbopaloobop alopbamboom," is a parody of sorts on the Pentecostal practice of speaking in tongues.[3]

Rock 'n' roll was a natural medium for radically personal expressions of redemption. While classical aesthetics emphasize the objective forms of musical compositions, rock aesthetics are centered more on the subjectivity of the listener.[4] The classical conception of music

---

2. I, like Steve Turner, use the terms "rock 'n' roll" and "rock music" interchangeably and generically to denote everything from rap to rockabilly. See Steve Turner, *Hungry for Heaven: Rock 'n' Roll & the Search for Redemption* (Downers Grove, IL: InterVarsity Press, 1995).
3. Turner, *Hungry for Heaven*, 21.
4. Bruce Baugh, "Prolegomena to Any Aesthetics of Rock Music," *The Journal of Aesthetics and Art Criticism* 51, no. 1 (Winter 1993): 23.

sees musical form as reflective of the mathematical properties which serve as mediators between heaven and earth; thus the emphasis in classical music is the conforming of our sensibilities, dispositions, and inclinations toward the patterns of perfection entailed in the music. By contrast, rock music is far more concerned with the immediate effect on the listener, and as such, tends to overturn the objectivity of classical aesthetics.[5] While classical music focuses on objective form, rock music emphasizes subjective effect. Because its focus is on individual appeal, rock music is inherently subjective, and thus facilitates a powerful medium for expressing personal and individual intimacies and affections, as such were originally expressed in the Southern church.

There are two important points here. First, the founding fathers of rock 'n' roll recognized that the burgeoning rock industry turned its back on rock music's Christian roots, and it did so primarily through the secularization of the lyrics; loving Jesus was in effect replaced by loving a pretty woman. Secondly, what carried over into the rock music industry is what journalist Steve Turner calls rock 'n' roll's search for redemption: rock music has always emphasized the need to break away somehow from this fallen world. However, in Turner's words: "Ultimately it was the redemption *feel* rather than the redemptive *message* that Southern rock 'n' rollers took to the world."[6] Because of the secularizing tendencies, the fallen world from which we are to be redeemed was redefined as the social and cultural norms of the fifties generation; rock music remained redemptive, but God and Satan had nothing to do with it.

---

5. Baugh, "Prolegomena," 27, gives the example of Joe Cocker's rendition of "With a Little Help from My Friends," which in many respects is a radical deviation from the Beatles' original recording, and yet it was well received. Had a classical musician taken such liberties with, say, Bach's *Chaconne*, he would find that critics and audiences are not nearly so tolerant, since it is the score itself that sets the limitations.
6. Turner, *Hungry for Heaven*, 33.

4. The Rock 'n' Roll Body

One of the primary ways in which rock music rebelled against the fifties was through the creation of a distinctively rock 'n' roll body. The key property of rock music is its rhythm. Rooted in the Southern Pentecostal synthesis of African, blues, and gospel traditions, one of the original intended effects of rock music was the stimulation of the body for dancing. Hence, the body is of central importance in rock music. Again, this stands in stark contrast to the movement of the human body in classical ballet, where the body becomes in a sense pure form through the illusion of effortless weightlessness among the dancers.[7] The body is used to transcend the body. Conversely, in rock music, the body is radically affirmed and finds its own forms for rhythmic expression, such as head-banging, foot-stomping, and hip-gyrating.

These forms of rhythmic expression challenged the social and cultural mores of the fifties, particularly in relation to gender norms. For example, what made Elvis so strange originally is that he sang like a man, indeed a gospel singer, but he moved on stage like a woman, gyrating his legs and swirling his hips. Subsequently, the advent of men donning long, shaggy hair followed the British invasion as the default rock fashion. Thus, secularized rock 'n' roll from its very beginning entailed transgender-like qualities. And with the advent of the sixties era, it became a full-blown call to cultural and sexual revolution in favor of a secularized vision of the sovereign individual. Rock began to celebrate a fully secularized vision of life that placed the self at the center of the universe.

---

7. Baugh, "Prolegomena," 26.

5. Contemporary Christian Music: An Ambiguous Reunion

Given its countercultural significance, it's not surprising that the wider church originally had serious problems with rock music. But this changed in the 1970s with the so-called Jesus Movement, which in effect readopted the musical forms of the counterculture movements as a means of evangelism and worship. With the founding of publishers such as *Maranatha! Music* and *Hillsong* and the rise of the praise band, the sounds of contemporary Christian worship began to take shape. Rock music had been restored to its place of origin.

However, while it might seem that rock 'n' roll simply came full circle back into the church, this reunion included some baggage acquired through rock music's industrial development, namely, the secularizing tendencies of the sovereign self. In other words, rock 'n' roll remained a powerful and profound call to redemption but now with the self at the center of life.

Today, it is ubiquitously believed that the self needs to be cultivated and nurtured, and in this process of turning toward the self, there has emerged a sense of entitlement to self-actualization, and an accompanying right to charge with malice anyone or anything that would seek to stifle the self. The result of this national collective self-indulgence is what researchers have called in a recent publication *The Narcissism Epidemic*. The authors of this study have noted "a single underlying shift in the American psychology: Not only are there more narcissists than ever, but non-narcissistic people are seduced by the increasing emphasis on material wealth, physical appearance, celebrity worship, and attention seeking."[8] It is precisely such a secularized self that risks forming and metastasizing in the worship of the contemporary church.

---

8. Jean M. Twenge and W. Keith Campbell, *The Narcissism Epidemic: Living in the Age of Entitlement* (New York: Atria, 2009), 1–2.

6. Privatized Space, Personal Faith

An objection to all of this may be: now wait a minute, the lyrics centering our minds on Jesus are able to overcome these secularizing tendencies, aren't they? Well, as it turns out, no they don't. And this is because Christianity in the West has experienced over the course of the last several decades what scholars call *privatization*, a process by which religious ideas and practices are relegated solely to the private sphere of life. The consequence of privatization, however inadvertent, is the loss of religion's objectivity. Because the private sphere of life involves subjective, optional, preferential, informal, and recreational dynamics, it offers no social support for objective, obligatory, formal, and unambiguous attributes for religious commitments. This is why it's so hard to defend the truth of Christianity today—because truth is public, not private; it's obligatory not optional; truth applies to all, not merely to some.

Theologian David F. Wells has traced extensively the effects of the privatization of Christian faith on the evangelical church. For Wells, what was once a moral age has transformed into a therapeutic age, characterized by "a confidence in self-mastery, the belief that the self can be reconstructed, that its aches and pains, its bewilderment, its confessions, can all be healed with the right technique."[9] It is in the context of such a transformation that the church's spirituality has undergone a comparable alteration, from classical to what he calls postmodern spirituality. "In classical spirituality," Wells writes, "access to God's presence is gained through believing his Word and trusting in the work of the Christ of that Word. . . . Access in postmodern spirituality . . . comes much more through the emotions and through bodily actions. The raising of hands, palms upward, the swaying to music, the arms outstretched to heaven, the release of inward emotion, this is what opens the door to the divine reality."[10]

---

9. David F. Wells, *Losing Our Virtue: Why the Church Must Recover Its Moral Vision* (Grand Rapids: Eerdmans Publishing, 1999), 186.
10. Wells, *Losing Our Virtue*, 43.

The privatization of the Christian church has thus inadvertently provided social support for the secularized self of rock 'n' roll and contemporary spirituality: what Jesus means to me personally is far more significant than what Jesus means objectively to the historic church.

Wells looks to the world of CCM for evidence of this shift in spirituality. While classical hymns focused on sin and the substitutionary death of Christ within a morally defined world, contemporary praise songs tend to reflect an amoral world wherein God provides psychological and therapeutic relief for the worshipper. He provides a particularly poignant example:

> He heard my cry and came to heal me,
> He took my pain and He relieved me,
> He filled my life and comforted me,
> And His name will shine, shine eternally.[11]

This psychologizing of sin is precisely the kind of permutation one would expect in a radically subjectivized world. This is why so much of contemporary Christian lyrics emphasize the first-person pronouns of me, myself, and I. Wells goes on to observe that among the contemporary praise songbooks he investigated, nearly 60 percent offered "no doctrinal grounding or explanation for the praise," in contrast to the classical hymnbooks where doctrinal grounding was virtually ubiquitous.[12]

The privatization of the Christian church has thus inadvertently provided social support for the secularized self of rock 'n' roll and contemporary spirituality: what Jesus means to me personally is far more significant than what Jesus means objectively to the historic church. Hence the ambiguity that I see inherent in CCM: on the

---

11. Jan Groth and Tore W. Aas, "His Name Will Shine," as cited in Wells, *Losing Our Virtue*, 42.
12. Wells, *Losing Our Virtue*, 44.

one hand, given its origins, it's an undeniably powerful medium for expressing our experience of redemption and longing for worship; on the other hand, it has imported and perpetuates significant subjectivity and secularity into the contemporary church. And therefore we shouldn't be surprised when our CCM artists and producers begin to exemplify secular sensibilities.

7. Redeeming CCM

Does this mean we need to get rid of CCM? As Christians, we are called to transfigure the totality of secular life through the transformative life, death, and resurrection of Christ, and this of course includes rock music.

So how should we go about this? What can we do to refine and secure CCM as a faithful means of celebrating a distinctively Christian vision of redemption?

There's plenty of good out there, we just need to make sure we're aware of the ambiguities of CCM given the secular currents so prominent in our age.

First, the church needs to challenge the secularized privatization of our faith. We have to recognize that we are not sovereign individuals; from the very moment of our conception, we are inescapably defined in terms of a relationship: we are either identified with the first Adam and therefore the old creation, or we are identified with the New Adam and therefore part of the New Creation, the return of Paradise in Christ. This relationality is the source of our personhood; the three persons of the Trinity are characterized by their relationships to one another. There is simply no such thing as privatized Christian faith.

Secondly, we need to reacquaint ourselves with a wider, more classical conception of music. In other words, we need to realize that music is *both* objective (as emphasized by the classical music tradition) *and* subjective (as emphasized by rock music). The focus on form and formality in classical music serves to awaken us to the transcendent and divine patterns of the cosmos to which we are called to conform our dispositions and inclinations. At the very least, the radically subjective elements of rock music in their immediate appeal to the body should be interpreted as part of larger cosmic frames of reference provided by a classical vision of music. An example would be classical African conceptions of rhythm, body, and dance, which envision the human body as a microcosm of the entire cosmos. African dance and ritual tend to appropriate music as a human means of joining in and maintaining the pulse of the cosmos.[13] Thus, we affirm the musical subjectivity of the body, but recognize that music itself can't be reductively relativized solely to the subjective.

Thirdly, the church should embrace those composers who recognize the powerful redemptive expression of rock music while completely rejecting the sovereign individual. I'm thinking particularly of people like Bob Kauflin, Chris Tomlin, and Keith and Kristin Getty, whose lyrics are theologically rich and passionate expressions of redemption without any defaulting to the therapeutic, the subjective, and the psychological that can be so characteristic of CCM today. In fact, I use Chris Tomlin's song "Indescribable" to introduce my students to something called *apophatic* theology, a theology of negation that talks about God in terms of what he's not. Tomlin's lyrics feature apophatic terms, such as "indescribable," "uncontainable," and "untamable," which describe God using negations; his greatness is beyond any human comprehension (cf. infinite, invisible, etc.). Chris Tomlin's song expresses this apophatic theology beautifully. So there's plenty of good out there, we just

---

13. See, for example, Alphonse Tiérou, *Dooplé: The Eternal Law of African Dance* (New York: Routledge, 1992), 17.

 Chapter Six. Rock 'n' Roll Music and the Church: A Morally Ambiguous Reunion

need to make sure we're aware of the ambiguities of CCM given the secular currents so prominent in our age.

If we are faithful in calling the sovereign self to repentance, then I believe we will begin to see the dissipation of secular norms as a whole, and the redeeming of every aspect of modern life, most especially rock 'n' roll.

QUESTIONS FOR REFLECTION AND DISCUSSION

1. Does your church worship with traditional hymnody, CCM, or a blend? Can you discern any correspondence between the music your church uses and other factors, such as the clothing worn by parishioners and the surrounding church architecture?

2. Name some of your favorite rock songs. What is it about them that you like so much?

3. Do you think your favorite rock songs, with lyrical modification, belong in Christian worship? Why or why not?

4. What are some examples in the Bible where different music is used in different contexts?

5. Do you agree that a rock 'n' roll aesthetic centers on the song's appeal to the body?

6. What are some other ways in which rock stars began transcending gender norms?

7. Read the lyrics of an eighteenth-century hymn and then the lyrics of a contemporary praise song. What are the similarities and differences between the two, and how would you account particularly for the differences?

8. How can rock music and CCM flourish in a Christian context? What changes, if any, would need to be made?

Suggested Listening Exercise

Listen to an older hymn in both its original version and a CCM arrangement. Reflect on the differences between the two performances. What do those differences tell us about the changes in time and culture between the original and its contemporary version? Does one focus on corporate singing, while the other focuses more on the individual?

Suggestions for Further Reading

Bruce Baugh, "Prolegomena to Any Aesthetics of Rock Music," *The Journal of Aesthetics and Art Criticism* 51, no. 1 (Winter 1993): 23–29.

Nik Cohn, *Awopbopaloobop Alopbamboom: The Golden Age of Rock* (New York: Grove Press, 1969).

John Frame, *Contemporary Worship Music: A Biblical Defense* (Phillipsburg, NJ: P&R Publishing, 1997).

Jay R. Howard and John M. Streck, *Apostles of Rock: The Splintered World of Contemporary Christian Music* (Lexington: University Press of Kentucky, 1999).

Steve Turner, *Hungry for Heaven: Rock 'n' Roll & the Search for Redemption* (Downers Grove, IL: InterVarsity Press, 1995).

David F. Wells, *Losing Our Virtue: Why the Church Must Recover Its Moral Vision* (Grand Rapids: Eerdmans Publishing, 1999).

Chapter Seven
Echoes of Eternity: Summary

We are now in a position to take stock of what we've learned thus far in our rediscovery of music. There are five major takeaways from our exploration.

First, music is *revelatory*. Like the wider world of sound, music discloses to our senses—indeed, to our entire bodies—an unseen reality, an otherwise imperceptible world. This revelatory significance renders music highly mystical, as evidenced by music's cross-cultural capacity to communicate the supernatural in rituals around the world. It's thus no coincidence that it is the only art or craft in the West named after a divinity, the Muses.

In reuniting heaven and earth, Christ restores the angelic sounds of Paradise in our midst, with the soundscape of the church providing the sonic witness that in Christ all things are made new.

Secondly, music is *cosmic* in nature. For the Greeks, Jews, and Christians, the revelatory significance of music involved manifesting on earth the music of the heavens, that is, the mathematical symmetries and consonances that constitute a harmonious cosmos. For the Greeks in particular, music resounded the mathematical principles of perfection upon which the cosmos was modeled. And in the Jewish temple, sacred music invoked the presence of God, the Lord of heaven and earth. Early Christians drew from both Greek and Jewish traditions in the formation of their own music theory and practice.

Thirdly, music is *moral*. The acoustic revelation of divine meaning and purpose served to cultivate wisdom and virtue within the listener, who thereby participated in the harmony of the cosmos, thus becoming truly human. For the Pythagorean tradition, the link between sound and mathematics provided the means by which the music of the spheres, otherwise imperceptible, could be reproduced on earth, thus transforming its listeners into heavenly beings.

Fourthly, music is *redeemed*. Christians transfigured this cosmic vision of music found among the Jews and Greeks by reenvisioning it as incorporated into the transformative life, death, and resurrection of Christ. In reuniting heaven and earth, Christ restores the angelic sounds of Paradise in our midst, with the soundscape of the church providing the sonic witness that in Christ all things are made new.

Fifthly, contemporary Christian music is *morally ambiguous*. Rock 'n' roll music developed from the unique demographic mixture of the church in the American South. While rock's emphasis on the subjective body rendered it a powerful form of worship, such subjectivity also left it vulnerable to moral relativism. This moral ambiguity has to be understood for the church to offer powerfully subjective worship music while maintaining the moral objectivity necessary for the cultivation of wisdom and virtue.

And so, having acquired a new conceptual vocabulary by which to hear, speak of, and share music, how shall we *apply* what we've learned to the *practice* of music? How can we better teach our students to listen to music with a well-trained and discerning ear, that they might hear and understand? How can our musical theology transfigure into actual music making?

Answers to these questions will occupy the remaining pages of our musical rediscoveries.

                    Chapter Seven. Echoes of Eternity: Summary

PART III
Music Practice

Chapter Eight
The Art of Listening:
The Practical Aesthetics of Music

Just as each note in a tune only makes sense in relation to the notes that precede and proceed from it, so music teaches us to understand each particular moment in our lives in relation to the unfolding of the whole.

1. Introduction

In his 1938 essay on the sociology of art, German sociologist and musician Theodor W. Adorno lamented what he called the "regression of listening" that had, in his mind, adversely infected American culture.[1] Adorno argued that the dominant consumerist culture of modern America had assimilated its inhabitants into a very different orientation toward the world, one in which our capacities for critical thinking have been subsumed under a tyranny of immediate gratification. Music, along with the whole of American cultural life, has been radically commodified and, as such, stripped of its capacity to interpret our immediate experiences in light of a larger reality. Just as each note in a tune only makes sense in relation to the notes that precede and proceed from it, so music teaches us to understand each particular

---

1. Theodor W. Adorno, "On the Fetish-Character in Music and the Regression of Listening," in *The Essential Frankfurt School Reader*, ed. Andrew Arato and Eike Gebhardt (New York: Continuum, 1985), 270–299.

moment in our lives in relation to the unfolding of the whole. Music teaches us to see diversity in relation to an overall unity, the fleeting in view of the enduring, and subjective harmonized with the objective. Instead, as consumers, we are caught up in the tyranny of the immediate, such that our inability to listen to music and all that it has to offer is indicative of our increasing disability to understand the fundamental questions of life and the moral obligations entailed therein.

If Adorno's critique sustains scrutiny, then our capacities for listening are highly consequential for our humanity. And so, I want to explore some of the practical dimensions of music, particularly as they relate to discerning and appreciating the aesthetics of musical composition and performance. What are the ways in which we ought to listen to music? How do we evaluate a musical piece? What should we be listening for? How do we access and interpret the ways in which music communicates meaning to our lives?

2. Musical Analysis

According to Roger Scruton, musical analysis "attempts to build a bridge from the sound structure to the aesthetic experience."[2] This bridge is built by accounting for what we might call the *Affekt* or emotional stimulations of a particular piece of music in its various compositional features. I have found John Hodges's threefold taxonomy quite helpful in constructing this correspondence. He recommends that we evaluate music on three levels: *performance*, *composition*, and *content*.[3] The first level involves the technical execution of the piece: How was it played? Was the piece executed with the requisite technical skill? Composition involves hearing the variant components of the piece individually as well as how they coalesce together. What are the features of its

2. Scruton, *Aesthetics*, 396.
3. John Mason Hodges, "Beauty in Music: Inspiration and Excellence," http://capress.link/ eoe0801.

melody? What is its time signature? How do the melody and rhythm correspond? What is the piece's harmonic structure? Does it change keys, and how is the melodic development affected? If there are lyrics, how does the composer "paint" the lyrics with melodic, rhythmic, and/or harmonic effect? Finally, Hodges recommends that we examine the content or *worldview* aspect of the musical piece. What does the composition say about the world in which we live? Is it a world filled with meaning and purpose? Is our world a moral one? Or is it amoral, devoid of any meaning or purpose?

Our central focus will be on the second of Hodges's analysis schema, the compositional character of the piece. We will in turn touch on the worldview component of the piece.

3. The Sounds of Spring

For our evaluation, we will explore the first movement of Vivaldi's violin concerto entitled *La Primavera*, or *Spring*. Vivaldi's concerto is based on an Italian sonnet[4] that reads:

> *Joyful spring has arrived,*
> *the birds greet it with their cheerful song,*
> *and the brooks in the gentle breezes*
> *flow with a sweet murmur.*
> *The sky is covered with a black mantle,*
> *and thunder and lightning announce a storm.*
> *When they fall silent, the little birds*
> *take up again their melodious song.*

After listening to the first movement, there are a number of musical constituents that come to the fore. Played in 4/4 time, the

---

4. Given that we don't know the author of the sonnet or the date of its composition, there is controversy as to whether the writing of the sonnet precedes Vivaldi's composition or whether it was written afterward. Some have speculated that Vivaldi himself may have written it. Regardless, it is widely accepted that the sonnets help us interpret the detailed nuances of the concertos. See Paul Everett, *Vivaldi: The Four Seasons and Other Concertos, Op. 8* (Cambridge: Cambridge University Press, 1996), 76.

piece exemplifies an elegant baroque instrumental texture of stringed instruments and harpsichord. We hear the key of E major established in the opening notes of the melody, which emphasizes the third and the fifth of an E major triad. This light and joyful introductory theme is then answered by another phrase, wherein the emphasis on the fifth of the E major triad causes the melody to climb upward, giving the piece direction and movement. The directional gesture of melodic ascent evokes a sense of growth, of things moving upward, such as a rising sun, budding flowers, and flying birds. This is a tonal depiction of the first line of the stanza, *Spring has arrived*.

Next, about thirty seconds in, a solo violin enters, with high-pitched trills that mimic the singing of birds. Other violins join in to create the effect of numerous birds chirping and tweeting through-out the countryside. The springtide of birdsong is then wrapped up with the answering theme at the beginning played by the whole string orchestra, thereby creating a sense of form and return, techni-cally known as *ritornello*, or "little return."

The return of the theme serves as the occasion for another develop-ment in the piece, this time an increased rhythm occasioned by a series of sixteenth notes in the form of an ostinato. The tones are moving along, flowing like a river ("the brooks in the gentle breezes flow"), progressively rising, while the violins pick up a breeze-like melody. As was the case with birdsong above, this section culminates in a return of the main theme, but notice that the register has changed; the melodic notes have been lowered to the dominant key (B). The piece is going on a journey; its har-mony is modulating, which means that the melodic breeze of the violins have swept us up and away from our tonal home. The piece is telling a story; a plot is developing and all the tensions bound up with such.

Next, with the advent of the second violin solo, we hear the rushing in of storm winds as per the text of the sonnet above ("The sky is covered with a black mantle, and thunder and lightning announce a storm"). Notice how the effect is achieved through a combination of tremolo, an increase in the rapidity of notes, as well as a melodic ascent to depict the storm coming nearer, and then a descent, as if to depict the sounds of heavy winds and rainfall dropping to the ground. The rapid tremolo culminates in a restatement of the opening theme, but now in a minor key: the storm has arrived.

The third violin solo depicts the sense of a storm's aftermath, with the original sounds of spring slowly coming back to life, as the melodies rise upward toward the in-breaking of the sun. This melodic ascent journeys back to its original key and then to the original theme, which rounds off the movement by bringing us back to our harmonic and melodic home.

4. The Architecture of Analysis

Our musical analysis involves several features that we can now delineate into a schema that can be used for musical evaluation in general.

a. Melodic analysis

Most musical pieces will have what is called a *theme* or *motif*, such as what we hear with the chorus in pop music. A motif is in many respects the heart of the music, the axle around which all the spokes of the song revolve, and is the most memorable part of the piece. You can describe the motif in a number of ways: 1) What is the melody's *direction*? Is it ascending or descending, and/or how is it directionally balanced? Does the melody develop in an ascending or descending fashion? 2) What is the melody's *range*? What are the lowest and highest notes? 3) What is the melody's *character*? Does it move stepwise in short intervals, or does it involve large intervallic leaps? 4) What is the melody's *contour*? What is the overall effect or *Affekt*[5] of the melodic direction, range, and character?

---

5. The term *Affekt* refers here to how human emotional expressions can be depicted or conveyed through musical gesture and arrangement.

Moreover, you can ask: Why does the melody have the contour that it does? Are there lyrics that are being emphasized or "painted" in a certain melodic way (we'll develop this below)? Does the melody go through any kind of variation throughout the piece? Is it altered in terms of its rhythm or syncopation, and/or does it go through any kind of harmonic change, as from a major key to a minor key? What was the difference between the last time you heard the theme and the first time? How did its placement at the end of the piece change the theme's feel and effect?

b. Harmonic analysis

In our analysis above, we began with an observation that the piece was in the key of E major. The important aspect of key is that it establishes harmonically our tonal *home*. In chapters 3 and 7, we discovered what Begbie refers to as the *teleological principles* of music, wherein the harmonic progressions in a piece generate a sense that the music is going somewhere. When we listen to a song, we inevitably anticipate a destination, as if the song were leading us to some kind of goal. Begbie notes that this teleological dynamic is generated primarily through a temporal structure that he describes as "equilibrium-tension-resolution." A song begins at a tonal *home*, what we call the *key*, and then the music *departs*—it goes on a journey—and that journey is marked by a kind of *tension*, a tension that arises from the dissonance of sensing that we are far away from home. But tonal music will always *resolve* that tension by bringing us back home, back to where we belong.

As with the Vivaldi piece, analyzing music involves explaining the harmonic journey that the musical piece is taking us on. How does the composer establish our tonal home? How and when did the piece give us a sense that we had moved away from such a home? How did the composer create tension? Was it associated with a particular lyric? In what ways were its repeated choruses different if they were represented in a different key or mode?

c. Rhythmic analysis

The rhythm of a piece provides the experience of coalescence; it provides a sense of temporal coherence.[6] This coherence is heard first in its meter, such as duple or quadruple meter (cf. "Twinkle, Twinkle, Little Star") and triple meter (the "Star-Spangled Banner" or any waltz). The rhythm may accent certain beats and create a sense of syncopation. Take note of any subdivisions of rhythms in between beats. For example, "Row, Row, Row Your Boat" is more or less a single note per beat, but then turns into a triplet subdivision associated with the lyrics "merrily, merrily, merrily." Notice how the triplets instantiate a rhythmic sense of merriment. And, of course, be aware of the tempo and its effect on the overall feel of the piece.

Moreover, you may have noticed that in the Vivaldi example, we didn't focus solely on the duration of tones, or even the meter; we were also aware of its rhythmic *form*, the ways in which the music moved toward certain fixed points, such as the ritornellos and the tremolos that transitioned to the minor key midway through. In this sense, the rhythm helped pave the way for our harmonic and melodic journey.

d. Combinations

More broadly, the question of evaluation involves reflecting on how well the melodic, rhythmic, and harmonic elements of the musical piece integrate with one another. Note how melody and rhythm so often come together in the Vivaldi piece to form *gestures*, which metaphorically evoke images in our minds and emotions in our hearts. What kind of melodic gestures do the rhythms display, and how are the melody and harmony integrally related? Is the harmony merely backup to the melody, or is it itself the manifestation of the interaction between a number of contrapuntal melodies? Is there a balance between the vertical (harmonic) and the horizontal (melodic) aspects of the piece? For example, Handel's music tends to

---

6. Scruton, *Aesthetics*, 338.

focus on the soprano and bass lines in terms of independent melodic movements, while the alto and tenor remain rather melodically uninteresting, functioning more as harmonic fillers. Bach, on the other hand, interweaves integrally independent melodies in each part into a harmonic tapestry.

Note too how the theme in Vivaldi's *Spring* could open up into all kinds of new possibilities. The melody creates space for the singing of birds; its majestic eighth-note pattern can transfigure into faster ostinato patterns; and the melody sounds as beautiful in a minor key as in a major key. The melody also allows for the music to slow down and speed up. Like creation itself, the theme is a seed that blossoms into innumerable creative possibilities.

e. Tone painting

Also known as *word* or *text painting*, this compositional technique involves depicting musically the meaning of lyrics. This means that if there are lyrics, we need to discern the ways in which the composer sonically shapes the words or concepts. Vivaldi does this indirectly insofar as *Spring* imitates the words of the sonnet upon which the music is based. But songs with lyrics may have a direct connection between the words and melody. For example, William Byrd's *Sanctus* ("Holy, Holy, Holy") for four voices starts the singing on a single note that then climbs upward and heavenward, mimicking the ascent of prayer. Bach's first series of melodic notes of the *Kyrie Eleison* from his incomparable *Mass in B Minor* also ascend into the heavens. Composers can devise ironic plays on words as well. In the "His Yoke Is Easy, His Burden Is Light" movement from his classic oratorio, *The Messiah*, Handel paints the word "easy" a melodic melisma that forces the voice to sing several sixteenth notes in quick succession; in other words, there isn't anything "easy" about it. Similarly, in the song "A Spoonful of Sugar" from the film score to *Mary Poppins*, the intervallic leap between the initial words "go down" . . . goes up!

And so, with word painting, we ask questions such as: In what ways are the words colored textually? Does the music become sad at the moment the lyrics are sad, or exuberant with exalting words? How does the melody express the emotion that the lyrics resemble? Said differently—we don't want to merely ask *what* is going on musically, but *why* is it going on? Why is the composer doing what he or she is doing at that moment?

Another application of tone painting is in the use of instrumental timbre. What kind of instruments are used and why? What does the color or timbre of the instrument add to the character of the melody or harmonies? Think, for example, of the ways in which the various instruments in Prokofiev's *Peter and the Wolf* are able to mimic uniquely the different features of the characters: the lightness of the strings represent the youthfulness of Peter; the high-pitched flute mimics the bird; the bassoon's low and buzzy tones evoke an elderly grandfather; the slinky sound of the clarinet depicts the smooth movements of a cat; and, of course, the low and heavy tones of horns depict the menacing presence of the wolf.

f. Worldview and lifeworld

A worldview does more than merely communicate the composer's conception of the world; the worldview is an *invitation* to experience the world in a very particular way, and thus to *share* in an experience indicative of a larger lifeworld. For example, Vivaldi's *Spring* is made up of musical gestures and forms that not only exemplify a world of order and loveliness, but also invite us to *delight* in creation, to *love* that world of order and loveliness. This is comparable to what theologian David Bentley Hart has observed about the music of Bach:

> Bach is the greatest of Christian theologians, the most
> inspired witness to the *ordo amoris* in the fabric of
> being; not only is no other composer capable of more
> freely developing lines or of more elaborate structures

of tonal mediation . . . but no one as compellingly demonstrates that the infinite is beauty and that beauty is infinite. It is in Bach's music, as nowhere else, that the potential boundlessness of thematic development becomes manifest: how a theme can unfold inexorably through difference, while remaining continuous in each moment of repetition, upon a potentially infinite surface of varied repetition. . . . Bach's is the ultimate Christian music; it reflects as no other human artifact ever has or could the Christian vision of creation.[7]

Contrast these features with, for example, the piece entitled *Philomel* by American composer Milton Babbitt. Written in 1964, it is a serial atonal work devoid of any discernible harmonic center; there is no distinguishable melody or rhythm; the vocal line appears radically random; and its computer-generated sounds leave the piece instrumentally vapid and sterile. So what is being communicated here? Is this Babbitt's vision of the world? Is life really this random, or is its order disguised by a seeming randomness? Is there anything lovely or redeeming about this piece? Are we being invited to share in this atonality as somehow normative?

> *Music can stimulate reactions from the listener in two ways: music can either* evoke *the listener to imitate musical gestures and expressions on the one hand, or it can* provoke *a reaction by forcing itself on the listener on the other.*

In contemplating this summoning aspect of music, I have found an essay by Roger Scruton, "Soul Music," exceptionally helpful.[8] Music can stimulate reactions from the listener in two ways: music can either *evoke* the listener to imitate musical gestures and expres-

---

7. David Bentley Hart, *The Beauty of the Infinite: The Aesthetics of Christian Truth* (Grand Rapids: Eerdmans, 2003), 282–283.
8. The article is available at http://capress.link/eoe0802.

     Chapter Eight. The Art of Listening: The Practical Aesthetics of Music

sions on the one hand, or it can *provoke* a reaction by forcing itself on the listener on the other. With the former, music is comprised of gestures and expressions that invite the listener to participate and imitate. Scruton uses the example of classical dance, where the participants dance *with* one another in bodily response to the rhythmic movements of the melodic lines. However, Scruton sees much pop music as more provoking response rather than evoking, such as the way laughter is triggered by tickling. The response to tickling is, in Scruton's words, "laughter without amusement"; it is purely reflexive rather than reflective. Scruton sees the radical emphasis on beat and volume in much pop music, together with its dissolution of melody and rhythm or even the dissipation of melody altogether (as in the case of thrash metal) as erasing the imitative nature of music. Here, music is no longer a proper object of movement that inspires a sympathetic response. And so, much popular dance today involves the participants dancing not *with* each other but *at* each other as part of the reactive nature of the music.

Plato's vision of music stalks Scruton's essay. We saw earlier in chapter 4 how Plato understood music as a primary means by which rhythm and harmony could be communicated through the body and sunk deeply into the recesses of the soul. For Plato, good music always involves the awakening of *arête*, the virtue of loving what is truly lovely and desiring what is truly desirable, and hence realizing our true humanity (cf. *Republic* 442A). "There is no doubt," writes Scruton,

> that music, for Plato, was something that could be judged in the same moral terms we judge one another, and that the terms in question denoted virtues and vices like nobility, dignity, temperance, and chastity on the one hand, and sensuality, belligerence, and indiscipline on the other.[9]

9. Roger Scruton, "Soul Music," *The American*, February 27, 2010, http://capress.link/ eoe0802.

Given the above distinction between evocation and provocation, reflection and reflex, it is difficult to disagree with Plato's view of music. All music invites us into a lifeworld through highly influential shaping mechanisms, evoking or provoking, sanctifying or desecrating.

5. SUMMARY

Adorno's lament over what he called the "regression of listening" has profound implications for our humanity. For, as we noted earlier, the fundamental questions of life are not answered by seeing as much as they are by hearing, by listening. If we in the modern age have lost such an aural reception, we in turn have cut ourselves off from a source indispensable to the formation of our humanity.

If we are ever to become once again, in Scruton's words, a "listening culture," we must at least in part recover the capacity to hear and respond to the formative aspects of music. To accept the invitation, we must first discern the invite as such. By accounting for the aesthetic experience of music; by discerning the interplay between its melodic, harmonic, and rhythmic components; by discovering the interrelationship between gesture and meaning, as well as the deeply formative nature of song, we discover the meaning of music—and in so doing, we unearth the mystery of life.

QUESTIONS FOR REFLECTION AND DISCUSSION

1. What do you think of Adorno's critique of a "regression of listening" in contemporary American culture? Hearken back to our discussion on visualism in chapter 1; how might such a regression affect adversely our conception of life?

2. Think of some of your favorite melodies and then evaluate them with the melodic analysis provided. What are their various features? How do they relate the melodies with their respective rhythms to create distinctive musical gestures?

3. Listen to another musical piece and apply the same architecture of analysis for your evaluation. What were the results? Did you hear similar characteristics as with the Vivaldi piece? What features did you find more prominent? Were you able to discern a worldview and lifeworld revealed through the music?

SUGGESTED LISTENING EXERCISE

Listen to the first movement of Vivaldi's violin concerto, *La Primavera*, or *Spring*, from his *Four Seasons* and apply the musical analysis listed above. Try other musical examples, even contemporary ones, and describe the kind of musical gestures you hear in each selection.

SUGGESTIONS FOR FURTHER READING

Helen Epstein, *Music Talks: Conversations with Musicians* (New York: Penguin Books, 1987).

Gary Gutting, "Mozart vs. the Beatles," http://capress.link/ eoe0803.

David Bentley Hart, "The Music of Eternity," http://capress.link/ eoe0804.

Paul Munson and Joshua Farris Drake, *Art and Music: A Student's Guide* (Wheaton, IL: Crossway, 2014).

Igor Stravinsky, *The Poetics of Music: In the Form of Six Lessons* (Cambridge, MA: Harvard University Press, 1970).

CHAPTER NINE
O 'Twas a Joyful Sound We Hear:
On Singing Psalms

1. INTRODUCTION

I walk into my classroom at the beginning of class, coffee in hand. About fifteen high school sophomores are gathered, standing around in a circle. At first glance it may appear that they are grouped according to gender, but closer inspection finds that they are actually grouped by vocal part: sopranos, altos, tenors, and, closest to me, basses. I take my psalter off the shelf and place it on the lectern. At this point, the lobbying begins. "Let's do Psalm 119X," one student requests. "No, we sang that just the other day," comes the protest from another. "How about 40E?" We decide on the psalm for the day and, after humming their starting notes, we begin to fill the room with the echoes of Paradise.

I am an educator. At the high school level, I teach students whose ages range from thirteen to nineteen, and at the university, eighteen to twenty-two. One of the differences in my pedagogical approach which is influenced by both logistics and training is that with the high schoolers I sing psalms. I am not at all exaggerating when I say, as an educator, that perhaps the most important parts of the school day are the times at the beginning of class when we sing psalms. This is because singing entails the power to create sacred space, a sanctified environment that can in turn sanctify all that goes on subsequently in the classroom. Singing harmonizes not merely the environment of the student, but the students themselves, bringing them in harmony with one another (you can't fight while you're singing together) and with themselves.

But more so, there is a profound harmonization *with the historic church* when we sing psalms together. This practice was not lost on the early and medieval church, nor was it neglected by the Protestant Reformers and the Puritans. Indeed, psalm singing is such an integral constituent to historic Christian identity that it is a wonder it could ever have been lost.

By singing the Psalms, we are not merely encountering Scripture; we are identified *with it.*

But lost it has become. In our day, the psalter is read far more than it is sung, an ironic departure from many of the Psalms' entailed instructions. And the four-part harmonies that our forefathers have bequeathed to us have been eclipsed by monophonic singing by musical illiterates who are guided by PowerPoint lyrics rather than musical notation. Lest I be mistaken for an elitist conservative curmudgeon, I think the consequences for this loss are profound. I believe that the loss of psalmody in our corporate, family, and private worship impoverishes significantly our sense of Scripture, our Christology, and our corporate identity as the people of God in this world. In fact, the more I sing through the psalter with my students and my own children, the more I am convinced that they learn more from singing than from any lecture I could give or reading I could assign. The church fathers discerned profound reasons for this, and it is these reasons that I would like to explore in what follows.

2. The Summary of Scripture

There is a longstanding tradition within the church that sees the
Psalms as an embodiment or summation of the Scriptures *en toto*.
For example, Basil of Caesarea wrote:

> All Scripture is inspired by God for our benefit; it
> was composed by the Spirit for this reason, that all we
> men, as if at a common surgery for souls, might each
> of us select a remedy for this particular malady. "Care,"
> it is said, "makes the greatest sin to cease." Now the
> Prophets teach certain things, the Historians and the
> Law teach others, and Proverbs provides still a different
> sort of advice, but the Book of Psalms encompasses
> the benefit of them all. It foretells what is to come and
> memorializes history; it legislates for life, gives advice
> on practical matters, and serves in general as a reposi-
> tory of good teachings, carefully searching out what is
> suitable for each individual. (*Homilia in psalmum i*)[1]

For Basil, to sing the Psalms is to be united melodically with the
sum total of biblical revelation. Ambrose the bishop of Milan concurred that the harmony of the Psalms embodies the harmony of all
Scripture: "History teaches, the Law instructs, prophecy proclaims,
reproach chastens and moralizing persuades; in the Book of Psalms
there is the successful accomplishment of all this along with a kind
of balm of human salvation" (*Explanatio psalmi I*, 7).[2] By singing the
Psalms, we are not merely encountering Scripture; we are *identified*
with it. In a very real way, our bodies transform into transmitters
of biblical revelation that send sacred messages in two directions:
toward others as we sing in harmony together, and toward ourselves,
as such harmony is produced by a collection of selves.

---

1. Cited in McKinnon, *Music*, 65.
2. Cited in McKinnon, *Music*, 126.

3. Christ's Own Prayers

For early Christians, the centrality of the Psalms for biblical faith appears rooted in an acute sense of the implications for the Incarnation. Jesus did not merely pray the Psalms; he embodied them. Their words were appropriated as his own. On the cross, his cry of dereliction (Ps. 22:1) and the committing of his spirit to the Father (Ps. 31:5) were spoken as endemic to himself. Similarly, the writer of Hebrews ascribed the words of Psalm 22:22 to Christ when he wrote: "*He* [Jesus] is not ashamed to call them brothers, saying, 'I will tell of your name to my brothers; in the midst of the congregation I will sing your praise'" (Heb. 2:11-12, NIV, emphasis mine). James E. Adams is correct when he observes: "Further intensive investigation bears out that the 'I,' the author of the Psalms, is Christ himself. His is the great voice we hear in the Psalms crying out in prayer to God the Father."[3]

> *When the Psalms are sung, not merely read, it brings the actions of the body, lungs, tongue, and lips in unison with the soul and the mind. The whole person is engaged in transmitting the songs of God.*

Augustine had a profound appreciation for the ecclesiastical significance of the prayer life of Jesus. He noticed that when the resurrected Christ confronted Paul (then Saul) on the road to Damascus, Jesus interrogated him about his persecution of the nascent church with the question: "Why are you persecuting *me?*" (Acts 9:4, emphasis mine). The psalmist's suffering voice is the suffering voice of Jesus precisely because our sufferings are now his by virtue of the Incarnation; having been incorporated into Christ, our temptations, pains, sorrows now become his, and he is thus able

---

3. James E. Adams, *War Psalms of the Prince of Peace: Lessons from the Imprecatory Psalms* (Phillipsburg, NJ: Presbyterian and Reformed Publishing, 1991), 25.

to bring to bear his own redeeming presence upon our fallenness. Moreover, when we sing the words of the psalmist, Christ's psalms become our psalms, his prayers are identified with our prayers.[4] We thus see revealed in the Psalms Christ in his genuine humanness, in his full participation in our sufferings and frustrations. In singing the book of Psalms, we therefore enter into the prayer world, the inner life, of the Incarnation.

4. HARMONY OF THE SOUL

As the Psalms harmonize the whole of Scripture in Christ, so they bring about a comparable harmony in the human person. The bishop of Alexandria, Athanasius (296–373), wrote an extended treatise reflecting on the ways in which the Psalms integrate the soul and body, where "Christians can find every aspect of their inner selves reflected, or more tellingly, revealed; every thought, every emotion, every feeling, every longing, every desire, every failing, foible and weakness."[5] When the Psalms are sung, not merely read, it brings the actions of the body, lungs, tongue, and lips in unison with the soul and the mind. The whole person is engaged in transmitting the songs of God.

Again, Ambrose concurred; he saw the Psalms as a holistic education for the formation of a virtuous soul:

> Whoever reads there [the Psalms], has a special remedy
> whereby he can cure the wounds of selfish passion.
> Whoever is willing to look closely, discovers a variety of
> contests prepared for him, as if in a communal gymna-
> sium of souls or a stadium of virtue, from which he can
> select for himself the one for which he knows himself
> best suited, in which he can more easily win the crown.

---

4. Rowan Williams, "Augustine and the Psalms," *Interpretation* 58, no. 1 (2004): 19.
5. Harrison, "Psalms Revisited," n.p.

If one is eager to study the deeds of our forebears and
wishes to imitate them, he finds contained within a
single psalm the entire range of ancestral history so
that he gains a treasury of memories as a stipend for his
reading. (*Explanatio psalmi* I, 7)[6]

Ambrose's psalmic perspective was certainly not lost on his
protégé, Augustine. The first line of his classic autobiography, *Confessions*, is a quotation from the Psalms (Ps. 47:2), and the Psalms serve
collectively to weave together his personal narrative through every
subsequent page. It has been observed that Augustine's autobiographical voice is systematically blended with the voice of the Psalms.[7]
Indeed, a psalm can be seen as a soul in microcosm, voicing the full
range of emotions buried within the human person in a conversation
with God. It is in the context of this conversation that the human person is radically transfigured in such a way that the recitation becomes
the instrument of transforming grace. "At the root of this understanding is the assumption that the grace of God changes what we *can* say
to God, and so changes what can be said of ourselves."[8]

5. Psalmody and Christian Culture

As instances of musical performance, the Psalms for Athanasius do
more than harmonize the self—they provide a mirror for the listener
to gaze at his own soul, such that the words of the Psalms become his
own: "It seems to me, moreover, that because the Psalms thus serve
him who sings them as a mirror, wherein he sees himself and his soul,
he cannot help but render them in such a manner that their words
go home with equal force to those who hear him sing, and stir them
also to a like reaction" (*Epistula ad Marcellinum*).[9] This is because

6. Cited in McKinnon, *Music*, 126.
7. Williams, "Augustine," 17.
8. Williams, "Augustine," 18.
9. Cited in Harrison, "Psalms Revisited," n.p.

corporate singing fosters a distinctively Christian soundscape that surrounds and incorporates the listener into this psalmody-based harmony as well: "those who do sing . . . so that the melody of the words springs naturally from the rhythm of the soul and her own union with the Spirit, they sing with the tongue and with the understanding also, and greatly benefit not themselves alone but also those who want to listen to them" (*Epistula ad Marcellinum*).[10]

> *Psalm singing, perhaps more than any other practice, fosters a distinctively Christian orientation toward the world from which a comparably Christian culture blossoms.*

The mutual singing of Psalms by its nature creates a sonically interrelated community. It has long been recognized that a singing people is a united people. We read in chapter 5 Ambrose's observation that psalmody "joins those with differences, unites those at odds and reconciles those who have been offended, for who will not concede to him with whom one sings to God in one voice?" (*Explanatio psalmi* I, 9).[11] Psalmody involves communion and thus entails a social order, which for Ambrose is the community of the Spirit. I think the early church fathers are quite correct on this. There is a reason why every political or social movement and every culture is expressed in corporate song. When we sing together, we are not merely claiming to create a social harmony and unity but also *demonstrating* social harmony. Our collective singing realizes and manifests tangibly in time and space the very Christological unity our hymns profess.

It is here that I have noticed one of the most significant effects of psalm singing on my students. We live in what has been called a consumerist age. This is an age in which students demand the pro-

---

10. Cited in Harrison, "Psalms Revisited," n.p.
11. Cited in Harrison, "Psalms Revisited," n.p.

fessor convince them that this class, or book, or subject material is worth their time and attention. When students become consumers, they stand in judgment over the class courses, and adopt an orientation toward education that becomes inherently sarcastic, flippant, and cynical.

In contrast, many students at our classical Christian school have learned through singing psalms and hymns to cultivate and conform their wants and desires to something greater than themselves. Such students grow to approach a particular class, book, or subject not just as something worth their time, but even as something of which we are not worthy. In such a cultivated classroom, students are not inclined to sink into arrogance or cynicism, but rather to regard their studies with wonder and awe. Psalm singing, perhaps more than any other practice, fosters a distinctively Christian orientation toward the world from which a comparably Christian culture blossoms.

Lest I be misunderstood, I certainly do not disparage hymnody or contemporary praise and worship. I do believe that the Holy Spirit is always inspiring new and dynamic ways of proclaiming the new creation in Christ through song as part of the church's ongoing enchanting witness. But certainly we can all agree that a song tradition common historically to all of the major branches of the church—Orthodox, Catholic, Protestant—and rooted in the prayer life of Christ himself should not be so sweepingly disregarded. Indeed, the Psalms are our inheritance, a treasure trove of biblical silver and Christological gold, which transfigures self and culture into pneumatic extensions of the Incarnation and thereby echoes Edenic life.

6. A New Generation of Psalm Singers

If you are unfamiliar with a psalter, I would suggest *The Book of Psalms for Singing,* published by Crown & Covenant, and the psalter-hymnal *Cantus Christi*, published by Canon Press. There are a number of resources that teach part singing as well, such as the Vanguard System (http://singinparts.com/). And if you don't read music, you need look no further than YouTube for a number of video instructionals on learning musical notation.

I am under no illusions over the difficulty of persuading others of what I have here envisioned. Ours is an age that reduces music to mere sentiment and entertainment, and as a result music no longer has the moral resources to make demands of its listeners. But I am convinced that a new generation of psalm singers is in fact emerging, one which will carry on this tradition in their melodies and harmonies, and in so doing, provide for the next generations a historical bridge to the songs of the saints of old, a sonic treasure trove that is our present and future inheritance.

QUESTIONS FOR REFLECTION AND DISCUSSION

1. What role have the Psalms played, or ought they to play, in your prayer life?

2. What are some Psalms that summarize the Old Testament?

3. How do Psalms 2, 89, and 110 foresee the ministry of the Messiah? How did Jesus Christ fulfill such expectations?

4. Why is it so important that we sing and not merely read the Psalms?

5. How are the Psalms indispensable for the formation of a distinctively Christian culture?

6. What steps can you take to give the Psalms more prominence in your own prayer life and school/homeschool culture?

Suggested Listening Exercises

There are two for this chapter. Watch this video of Shane & Shane singing Psalm 46: http://capress.link/eoe0901. In light of our discussion in chapter 6, reflect on how this contemporary psalm arrangement is an example of redeeming or resolving the ambiguities in CCM.

The next listening exercise will involve singing. Start learning psalms as part of your classroom content. Begin with just the melody, and slowly add different vocal parts. Notice how the various lines support and complement the melody line without overwhelming it. This is an example of how choirs were once considered exemplative of the ideal society.

Suggestions for Further Reading

James E. Adams, *War Psalms of the Prince of Peace: Lessons from the Imprecatory Psalms* (Phillipsburg, NJ: Presbyterian and Reformed Publishing, 1991).

Brian Daley, "Is Patristic Exegesis Still Usable? Reflections on Early Christian Interpretation of the Psalms," *Communio* 29 (Spring 2002): 185–216.

Lisa M. Hess, *Learning in a Musical Key: Insight for Theology in Performative Mode* (Eugene, OR: Pickwick Publications, 2011).

James B. Jordan, "How to Chant the Psalms," http://capress. link/eoe0902.

T.M. Moore, *The Psalms for Prayer* (Grand Rapids: Baker Books, 2002).

The Psalter: According to the Seventy, translated from the Septuagint by the Holy Transfiguration Monastery (Brookline, MA: Holy Transfiguration Monastery, 2008).

Willem A. VanGemeren, *Psalms*, vol. 5, *The Expositor's Bible Commentary, Revised Edition*, ed. Tremper Longman III and David E. Garland (Grand Rapids: Zondervan, 2008).

N.T. Wright, *The Case for the Psalms: Why They Are Essential* (New York: HarperOne), 2013.

POSTLUDE

Buildings crumble, books become brittle and damaged, and national borders rise and fall. But the frequencies that animate the melodic world of music are somehow permanent, unchanging, and endlessly enduring, particularly as they are caught up in the worship life of the church.

I now stand many years removed from those occasional evenings when I played the classical guitar for my grandfather. In the interludes between my exploring the attic and various rooms in his old Dutch colonial home and my outdoor adventures in the acreage of his backyard, I would tune my strings and perform for this veteran of World War I, this PhD chemist and one-time concert pianist.

He sat and listened, always attentively.

And in between the scales and arpeggios and the rhythmically shaped melodies and harmonies, he would comment on my performance, interposing his own wisdom gathered from a life that spanned nearly a century. Among his sagacious litanies, there was one maxim that stood out. My grandfather used to tell me that music, particularly classical music, was the only thing in this world that lasts forever. Perhaps this was a bit overstated; certainly, it is the church, the Bride of Christ, that lasts forever. But there's something to what my grandfather said. Buildings crumble, books become brittle and damaged, and national borders rise and fall. But the frequencies that animate the melodic world of music are somehow permanent, unchanging, and endlessly enduring, particularly as they are caught up in the worship life of the church.

His elderly wisdom was anticipated centuries earlier by the words of St. Ignatius of Antioch, who wrote: "He who carries God in his heart, bears heaven with him wherever he goes." I don't know if my grandfather was familiar with St. Ignatius, but I think he would enthusiastically approve, though with one caveat. It is through music that we so often sense the presence of God in our hearts; in the memories of life experiences swept up in melodies, in the time and space that provide music its canvas, in the singing communities that transform into social harmonies, in the depth of awakened emotions we never before dreamed were within us. He who melodically carries God in his heart, bears *eternity* within himself.

This was my grandfather's legacy that he left for me, even when the guitar was placed back into its case. It is an inheritance that has ever since oriented my life toward the sounds of Eden, which I hope to have shared with you in these few pages, that sonic fragrance floating on the breeze of divine grace. For there, in the echoes of eternity, dwells the song of Paradise, beckoning us, leading us, and calling us home.

APPENDIX A
Seven Ways to Incorporate Music throughout the School Day

We live in a music-saturated world. From waking up to radio-set alarm clocks, to the music piping out of our computers and iPods, to the musical ringtones on our smartphones, to the intercoms in our gas stations, restaurants, and malls, almost everything we practice throughout the day involves music.

We are a music-saturated world because humans are music-saturated creatures. It is in our nature to make music.

It is no wonder then that classical education puts a tremendous emphasis on music as a way of cultivating the senses of the body and training the virtues of the soul.

Unfortunately, I have to say that I think one of the great impoverishments in our schools is that the musical means of learning tends to die out after sixth or seventh grade. Chants fill the classrooms in the grammar school, only to be eclipsed by the lectern in the upper school, and we sequester singing to the specialization of the choir teacher.

We can hear the fruits of such specialization when our students resist participation in music by saying, "But I can't sing" or "I don't like singing." It is imperative that we underscore for them that they *ought* to; they ought to love to sing. And this is because they were created by and bear the image of the God who creates and sustains the world in a grand cosmic harmony. In short, we need to impress upon our students that they were *created* to sing.

Perhaps the most important thing we can be doing as educators to avoid compartmentalizing music is to teach our students to sing throughout the school day. I have seen the fruits of doing so in our own school. Nothing has contributed more to the formation of Christian culture in our school than the practice of regular intervals of daily singing.

And so, with this in mind, here are seven practical ways to effectively incorporate music throughout the school day:[1]

1. **Allocate certain times in the day for plenary singing and prayer.** We sing together as an entire upper school first thing in the morning, along with reciting corporate prayer. Students also sing together the Doxology at lunch, and sometimes at the end of the school day.

2. **Organize music according to the seasons.** We program the music and prayers in the morning according to the liturgical calendar (Advent, Christmas, Epiphany, Lent, and Easter). This gives students a sense of the rhythm of sacred time.

3. **Use music in Latin and Greek class.** This is a wonderful opportunity for students to learn Gregorian chant and the Greek octoechos, the eight tones, each representing a different spiritual state. There are a number of resources on the Web where you can print out musical notation for Latin and Greek chants.

4. **Begin/end class with singing.** Many classes at Christian schools begin with prayer. But I am not at all exaggerating when I say that as an educator, perhaps the most important parts of the school day are the times at the beginning of class when we sing psalms. This is because singing entails the power to create sacred space, a sanctified environment that can in turn sanctify all that goes on subsequently in the classroom. Singing harmonizes not merely the environment of the student, but the students themselves, bringing them

---

1. I want to thank my fellow Alcuin Fellowship member and musician Bill Stutzman of The Oaks Classical Christian Academy in Spokane, WA, for his wonderful suggestions.

in harmony with one another (you can't fight while you're singing together) and with themselves. Singing may also be appropriate at the end of class as a solidifying, doxological response to all that was learned.

5. **Learn to sing in parts.** Unison singing is fine (especially in the context of ancient chant). But singing in parts helps the students to understand themselves as embodying the unity in diversity in the fellowship of the Trinity. It also opens up to them a whole new world of historic psalm and hymn singing.

   There are a number of resources that teach part singing as well, such as the Vanguard System (http://singinparts.com/). And, as mentioned earlier, if you don't read music, you need look no further than YouTube for a number of video instructionals on learning musical notation.

6. **Choose good music as background.** Another way of cultivating the sonic beauty of your school is selecting good music as background for your studies. Background music can contribute to fostering a sense of sacred space for contemplating the True, the Good, and the Beautiful, and thereby provides an opportunity for students to cultivate an affection for music that nurtures the student virtues of attentiveness, observance, and inquiry.

7. **Incorporate music into the lesson plans of the wider curriculum.** Music can serve to illuminate thematically or historically various classroom lessons. Greg Wilbur has suggested that when reading the book of Exodus, have the students listen to portions of *Israel in Egypt* by G.F. Handel, or when studying Old Testament messianic expectations, listen to Handel's *Messiah*. For studies in the Middle Ages and Renaissance, listen to samples of Gregorian chant such as *Dies Irae* and the Renaissance polyphony of Josquin, Palestrina, and Tallis.[2]

---

2. See Gregory Wilbur, "A Foundation for Music Appreciation," *Classis* 17, no. 1 (Spring 2010): 11–13.

By incorporating music throughout the school day, you will not only cultivate the senses and foster the virtues of your students, but also develop community and camaraderie among students and teachers, awaken the beauty of Christian culture, and enhance the beauty of the school environment.

Now that's something to sing about!

SUGGESTED RESOURCES

The Book of Psalms for Singing (Pittsburgh: Crown & Covenant, 1998).

"Byzantine Chant," http://capress.link/eoeappa01.

Cantus Christi (Moscow, ID: Canon Press, 2004).

"How to Read and Sing Gregorian Chant," http://capress.link/eoeappa02.

Jarrod Richey, *Bach to the Future: Fostering Music Literacy Today* (Monroe, LA: Retune Publications, 2016).

The Vanguard System, http://singinparts.com/.

Appendix B
Time and Eternity:
The Sacred Soundscape of Arvo Pärt[1]

Arvo Pärt is considered by many to be the greatest living composer in our time. Beloved by rock stars, film producers, and documentary makers, his music comprises perhaps the single most sought-after sounds floating across the borders of classical music today.

Born September 11, 1935, in Soviet-dominated Estonia, Pärt studied musical composition at the Tallinn Conservatory. He instantly became a child of his age, learning and composing the avant-garde and serialist styles that were so fashionable among the intellectual elite.

But then Arvo Pärt hit a wall. Beginning in 1968, he went silent for almost ten years. It was during this time that he converted to Russian Orthodoxy and began studying in-depth the techniques and processes of early Christian music, particularly the unadorned melodic contours of plainchant, or what's more popularly known as Gregorian chant.

He then began experimenting with the sounds awakening from the intertwining of two melodic voices, which in turn became an Incarnational model for the whole of his subsequent works: a melody line that captures the adversities and struggles of this fallen world, and a melodic counterpoint of divine grace and healing that redeems and transfigures the pains and sorrows of our world.

---

1. This is the transcript from my podcast episode by the same title, available here: http://capress.link/eoeappb01.

Arvo Pärt's decade-long silence involved nothing less than his own return to a world filled with divine meaning and purpose, from which he forged a compositional technique that sonically reanimated that mystical world into our own, awakening us to the divine reality that surrounds us and yet remains eclipsed by the assumptions of a secular age.

Pärt called this new-ancient style of composition *tintinnabuli*, which means literally "the sound of a small bell." And with good reason: his music seems to mystically cascade from inside the purity of overtones resounding in such ringing.

Central to this compositional technique is Pärt's use of silence and space, which transform into the mystical canvas upon which his music floats. Pärt himself describes it this way:

> Time, for us, is like the time of our own lives. It is temporary. What is timeless is the time of eternal life; that is eternal. Like the sun, we cannot really look at it directly, but my intuition tells me that the human soul is closely connected to both of them, time and eternity.[2]

When listening to his music, you'll hear that Pärt often ends his phrases in a dissonance, without completed resolution; this compositional technique for Pärt represents the sins of humanity, which have distorted the world around us. And yet this dissonance is interwoven with melodies of divine grace and mercy, thus transfiguring his music into a sonic revelation of the incorporation of the entire cosmos into the transformative life, death, and resurrection of Christ.

The soundscape created by Arvo Pärt draws the listener into the rich and illustrious world of Russian Orthodox music, and as such, recovers the sacramental and indeed mystical nature of art and beauty. Far from our world's consumerist sensibilities, that render

---

2. Tom Huizenga, "The Silence and Awe of Arvo Pärt," *Morning Edition*, June 2, 2014, http:// capress.link/eoeappb02.

     Appendix B. Time and Eternity: The Sacred Soundscape of Arvo Pärt

music and art to a matter of mere personal preference and subjective taste, art and beauty were once considered bridges to another world—indeed, an eternal world that has broken into our own through the Incarnation of Christ and the restoration of the cosmos. Arvo Pärt's music invites us to reimagine our world in just such a way, wherein our desires are drawn toward heaven, into a divine communion in which all things are eternally perfected in God.

SUGGESTED LISTENING FOR ARVO PÄRT

Für Alina

Magnificat

Cantus in Memory of Benjamin Britten

"Sanctus" from the *Berlin Mass*

Spiegel im Spiegel

BIBLIOGRAPHY

Adams, James E. *War Psalms of the Prince of Peace: Lessons from the Imprecatory Psalms.* Phillipsburg, NJ: Presbyterian and Reformed Publishing, 1991.

Adams, John Luther. "In Search of an Ecology of Music." http://capress.link/eoe0302.

Adorno, Theodor W. "On the Fetish-Character in Music and the Regression of Listening." In *The Essential Frankfurt School Reader*, edited by Andrew Arato and Eike Gebhardt, 270–299. New York: Continuum, 1985.

Anttila, Miikka E. *Luther's Theology of Music: Spiritual Beauty and Pleasure.* Berlin: Walter de Gruyter, 2013.

Apocalypse of Abraham. http://capress.link/eoe0502.

Aristotle. *Politics.* Translated by H. Rackham. Loeb Classical Library. Cambridge: Harvard University Press, 1932.

Asante, Kariamu Welsh. *African Dance: An Artistic, Historical, and Philosophical Inquiry.* Trenton, NJ: Africa World Press, 1998.

Augustine. "*De Musica.*" *The Fathers of the Church, Vol. 4.* Translated by Robert Taliaferro. Washington, DC: Catholic University of America Press, 1947.

Bakan, Michael B. *World Music: Traditions and Transformations.* New York: McGraw-Hill, 2007.

Barker, Margaret. "Temple Music." http://capress.link/eoe0403.

Barker, Margaret. *Temple Themes in Christian Worship.* London: T&T Clark International, 2007.

Barnes, Paul. "Franz Liszt and the Sacramental Bridge: Music as Theology of Presence," http://capress.link/eoe0101.

Baugh, Bruce. "Prolegomena to Any Aesthetics of Rock Music." *The Journal of Aesthetics and Art Criticism* 51, no. 1 (Winter 1993): 23–29.

Beck, Guy L., ed. *Sacred Sound: Experiencing Music in World Religions.* Waterloo, Ontario: Wilfrid Laurier University Press, 2006.

Beck, Guy L. *Sonic Theology: Hinduism and Sacred Sound.* Columbia: University of South Carolina Press, 1993.

Begbie, Jeremy S. *Theology, Music and Time.* Cambridge: Cambridge University Press, 2000.

Begbie, Jeremy S., and Steven R. Guthrie, eds. *Resonant Witness: Conversations between Music and Theology*. Grand Rapids: Eerdmans, 2011.

Boethius. *The Consolation of Philosophy*. Translated by Richard H. Green. Mineola, NY: Dover Publications, 2002.

Boethius. *The Fundamentals of Music*. Translated by Calvin M. Bower. New Haven, CT: Yale University Press, 1989.

Borst, Arno. *The Ordering of Time: From the Ancient Computus to the Modern Computer*. Translated by Andrew Winnard. Chicago: University of Chicago Press, 1993.

Carson, Charles. "'Whole New Worlds': Music and the Disney Theme Park Experience." *Ethnomusicology Forum* 13, no. 2 (Nov. 2004): 228–235.

Cole, Basil. *Music and Morals: A Theological Appraisal of the Moral and Psychological Effects of Music*. Staten Island, NY: Alba House, 1993.

Daley, Brian. "Is Patristic Exegesis Still Usable? Reflections on Early Christian Interpretation of the Psalms." *Communio* 29 (Spring 2002): 185–216.

Dulles, Avery Cardinal. *A History of Apologetics*. Eugene, OR: Wipf and Stock Publishers, 1997.

Everett, Paul. *Vivaldi: The Four Seasons and Other Concertos, Op. 8*. Cambridge: Cambridge University Press, 1996.

Fabian, Johannes. *Time and the Other: How Anthropology Makes Its Object*. New York: Columbia University Press, 1983.

Fubini, Enrico. *The History of Music Aesthetics*. London: Macmillan, 1990.

Godwin, Joscelyn. *Harmonies of Heaven and Earth: The Spiritual Dimensions of Music from Antiquity to the Avant-Garde*. Rochester, VT: Inner Traditions International, 1987.

Godwin, Joscelyn, ed. *The Harmony of the Spheres: A Sourcebook of the Pythagorean Tradition in Music*. Rochester, VT: Inner Traditions International, 1993.

Gregory of Nyssa. *The Life of Moses*. Translated by Abraham J. Malherbe and Everett Ferguson. New York: Paulist Press, 1978.

Grout, Donald Jay, J. Peter Burkholder, and Claude V. Palisca. *A History of Western Music*. New York: Norton, 2001.

Harrison, Carol. *The Art of Listening in the Early Church*. Oxford: Oxford University Press, 2013.

Harrison, Carol. "Augustine and the Art of Music." In *Resonant Witness: Conversations between Music and Theology*, edited by Jeremy S. Begbie and Steve R. Guthrie, 27–45. Grand Rapids: Eerdmans, 2011.

Harrison, Carol. "Psalms Revisited." Unpublished paper.

Hart, David Bentley. *The Beauty of the Infinite: The Aesthetics of Christian Truth*. Grand Rapids: Eerdmans, 2003.

Heaney, Maeve Louise. *Music as Theology: What Music Says about the Word*. Eugene, OR: Pickwick Publications, 2012.

Hess, Lisa M. *Learning in a Musical Key: Insight for Theology in Performative Mode*. Eugene, OR: Pickwick Publications, 2011.

Hobbs, Gerald. "Christianity and Music." In *Sacred Sound: Experiencing Music in World Religions*, edited by Guy L. Beck, 61–88. Waterloo, Ontario: Wilfrid Laurier University Press, 2006.

Hodges, John Mason. "Beauty in Music: Inspiration and Excellence." http://capress.link/eoe0801.

Hodges, Richard. "Drum Is the Ear of God: Africa's Inner World of Music." http://capress.link/eoe0301.

Hoews, David, ed. *The Varieties of Sensory Experience: A Sourcebook in the Anthropology of the Senses*. Toronto: University of Toronto Press, 1991.

Huizenga, Tom. "The Silence and Awe of Arwo Pärt." *Morning Edition*, June 2, 2014. http://capress.link/eoeappb02.

Hull, John. *Touching the Rock: An Experience of Blindness*. London: SPCK, 1990.

Ihde, Don. *Listening and Voice: Phenomenologies of Sound*. Albany: State University of New York Press, 2007.

Johnson, Mark. *The Meaning of the Body: Aesthetics of Human Understanding*. Chicago: University of Chicago Press, 2012.

Jordan, James B. "How to Chant the Psalms." http://capress.link/eoe0902.

Köpping, Klaus-Peter, Bernhard Leistle, and Michael Rudolph, eds. *Ritual and Identity: Performative Practices as Effective Transformations of Social Reality*. Berlin: Lit Verlag, 2006.

Leithart, Peter J. *From Silence to Son: The Davidic Liturgical Revolution*. Moscow, ID: Canon Press, 2003.

Levin, Theodore C., and Michael E. Edgerton. "The Throat Singers of Tuva." *Scientific American* (Sept. 1999): 80–87.

Louth, Andrew. *The Origins of the Christian Mystical Tradition: From Plato to Denys*. Oxford: Oxford University Press, 1981.

Martin, Ralph P. "Aspects of Worship in the New Testament Church." *Vox Evangelica II* (1963): 6–32.

Martineau, Jason. *The Elements of Music: Melody, Rhythm, and Harmony*. New York: Bloomsbury, 2008.

McKinnon, James. *Music in Early Christian Literature*. Cambridge: Cambridge University Press, 1987.

Moore, T.M. *The Psalms for Prayer*. Grand Rapids: Baker Books, 2002.

Nancy, Jean-Luc. *Listening*. Translated by Charlotte Mandell. New York: Fordham University Press, 2007.

Otto, Rudolf. *The Idea of the Holy*. Translated by John W. Harvey. Oxford: Oxford University Press, 1950.

Plato. "Timaeus." Translated by R.G. Bury. *Plato, Vol. VII*. Loeb Classical Library. Cambridge: Harvard University Press, 1952.

The Psalter: According to the Seventy. Translated from the Septuagint by the Holy Transfiguration Monastery. Brookline, MA: Holy Transfiguration Monastery, 2008.

Quasten, Johannes. *Music and Worship in Pagan and Christian Antiquity*. Translated by Boniface Ramsey, O.P. Washington, DC: National Association of Pastoral Musicians, 1983.

Qureshi, Regula. "Islam and Music." In *Sacred Sound: Experiencing Music in World Religions*, edited by Guy L. Beck, 89–111. Waterloo, Ontario: Wilfrid Laurier University Press, 2006.

Rappaport, Roy A. *Ritual and Religion in the Making of Humanity*. Cambridge: Cambridge University Press, 1999.

Rée, Jonathan. *I See a Voice: A Philosophical History of Language, Deafness and the Senses*. New York: HarperCollins, 1999.

Reilly, Robert. "The Music of the Spheres." http://capress.link/eoe0404.

Richey, Jarrod. *Bach to the Future: Fostering Music Literacy Today*. Monroe, LA: Retune Publications, 2016.

Schopenhauer, Arthur. *The World as Will and Representation, Vol. 1*. Translated by E.F.J. Payne. Indian Hills, CO: Falcon's Wing Press, 1958.

Scruton, Roger. *The Aesthetics of Music*. Oxford: Clarendon Press, 1997.

Scruton, Roger. "Soul Music." *The American*, February 27, 2010. http://capress.link/eoe0802.

Shelemay, Kay Kaufman. *Soundscapes: Exploring Music in a Changing World*. New York: Norton, 2015.

Small, Christopher. *Musicking: The Meanings of Performing and Listening*. Middletown, CT: Wesleyan University Press, 1998.

Smith, John Arthur. *Music in Ancient Judaism and Early Christianity*. Farnham, Surrey: Ashgate, 2011.

Stone-Davis, Férdia J. *Musical Beauty: Negotiating the Boundary between Subject and Object*. Eugene, OR: Cascade Books, 2011.

The Testament of Adam. http://capress.link/eoe0501.

Tiérou, Alphonse. *Dooplé: The Eternal Law of African Dance*. New York: Routledge, 1992.

Turley, Stephen R. *Awakening Wonder: A Classical Guide to Truth, Goodness & Beauty*. Camp Hill, PA: Classical Academic Press, 2015.

Turner, Steve. *Hungry for Heaven: Rock 'n' Roll & the Search for Redemption.* Downers Grove, IL: InterVarsity Press, 1995.

Twenge, Jean M., and W. Keith Campbell. *The Narcissism Epidemic: Living in the Age of Entitlement.* New York: Atria, 2009.

Uzukwu, E. Elochukwu. *Worship as Body Language: Introduction to Christian Worship: An African Orientation.* Collegeville, MN: The Liturgical Press, 1997.

VanGemeren, Willem A. *Psalms.* Vol. 5 of *The Expositor's Bible Commentary, Revised Edition,* edited by Tremper Longman III and David E. Garland. Grand Rapids: Zondervan, 2008.

Vaziri, Mostafa. *Rumi and Shams' Silent Rebellion: Parallels with Vedanta, Buddhism, and Shaivism.* New York: Palgrave Macmillan, 2015.

Wannenwetsch, Bernd. "'Take Heed What Ye Hear': Listening as a Moral, Transcendental and Sacramental Act." *Journal for the Royal Musical Association* 135, no. S1 (2010): 91–102.

Warren, Rick. *The Purpose Driven Church: Growth without Compromising Your Message and Mission.* Grand Rapids: Zondervan, 1995.

Wellesz, Egon. *A History of Byzantine Music and Hymnography.* Oxford: Clarendon Press, 1961.

Wells, David F. *Losing Our Virtue: Why the Church Must Recover Its Moral Vision.* Grand Rapids: Eerdmans Publishing, 1999.

Wilbur, Gregory. "A Foundation for Music Appreciation," *Classis* 17, no. 1 (Spring 2010): 11–13.

Williams, Rowan. "Augustine and the Psalms." *Interpretation* 58, no. 1 (2004): 17–27.

Williams, Sean. "Buddhism and Music." In *Sacred Sound: Experiencing Music in World Religions,* edited by Guy L. Beck, 169–189. Waterloo, Ontario: Wilfrid Laurier University Press, 2006.

Wright, N.T. *The Case for the Psalms: Why They Are Essential.* New York: HarperOne, 2013.

About the Author

Steve Turley (PhD, Durham University) is an internationally recognized scholar, speaker, blogger, and prize-winning classical guitarist. He is the author of over ten books, including *Awakening Wonder: A Classical Guide to Truth, Goodness & Beauty* (Classical Academic Press) and *The Ritualized Revelation of the Messianic Age: Washings and Meals in Galatians and 1 Corinthians* (T&T Clark). Steve blogs on the church, society and culture, education, and the arts at TurleyTalks.com. He is a faculty member at Tall Oaks Classical School in Newark, DE, where he teaches theology, Greek, and rhetoric, and he is a professor of fine arts at Eastern University. Steve lectures at universities, conferences, and churches throughout the U.S. and abroad. His research and writings have appeared in such journals as *Christianity and Literature, Calvin Theological Journal, First Things, Touchstone,* and *The Chesterton Review,* and he is a regular contributor to *The Imaginative Conservative* and *The Christian Post.* Steve and his wife, Akiko, have four children and live in Newark, DE, where they together enjoy fishing, gardening, and watching *Duck Dynasty* marathons.

For more information on Steve, his books, videos, podcasts, and e-learning courses, please visit www.turleytalks.com.

The Classical Education Series Bundle
Receive all 3 for $19.95
reg. $26.85

An Introduction to Classical Education:
A Guide for Parents
by Christopher Perrin, PhD

A Student's Guide to Classical Education
by Zoë Perrin Endicott, BA English Literature

The Liberal Arts Tradition:
A Philosophy of Christian Classical Education
by Kevin Clark, DLS & Ravi Jain, MA

Recommended by the
International Journal of
Christianity & Education

ClassicalAcademicPress.com

Giants in the History of Education Bundle

Receive all 4 for $24.95
or $7.95 each

John Milton: Classical Learning and the Progress of Virtue
by Grant Horner, PhD

C.S. Lewis: An Apologist for Education
by Louis Markos, PhD

Plato: The Great Philosopher-Educator
by David Diener, PhD

John Amos Comenius: A Visionary Reformer of Schools
by David Smith, PhD

ClassicalAcademicPress.com

What are the best books your K–12 students should be reading?

Find out at:
ClassicalReader.com
Sort by grade, level, genre, and more!

CLASSICAL ACADEMIC
CAP

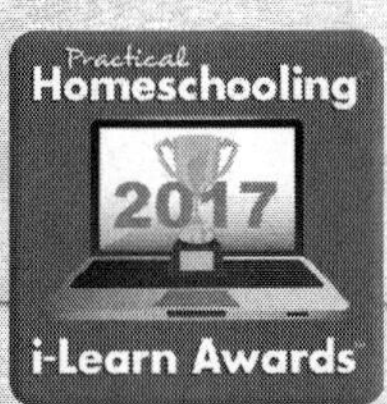

Live, online courses for grades 3–12 that are classical and restful, cultivating a deep engagement with learning.

- Latin • Logic • Writing • Rhetoric • Grammar
- History • Literature • Math • and more!

ScholeAcademy.com